Christina Dymock

One dirty BOWL

Fast Desserts • Faster Cleanup

Front Table Books • An Imprint of Cedar Fort, Inc. • Springville, Utah

ISBN 13: 978-1-4621-1401-6

Published by Front Table Books, an imprint of Cedar Fort, Inc.
2373 W. 700 S., Springville, UT 84663
Distributed by Cedar Fort, Inc., www.cedarfort.com

Library of Congress Cataloging-in-Publication Data on file

Cover and page design by Erica Dixon
Cover design © 2014 by Lyle Mortimer
Edited by Casey J. Winters

Printed in the United States of America

10 9 8 7 6 5 4 3 2 1

To Craig.

Thank you for washing dirty dishes, tasting my experiments, sending me out the door to book signings, and understanding how much writing means to me. You're amazing!

Contents

Welcome to One dirty BOWL

Fast Desserts • Faster Cleanup

There's something wonderful about presenting baked goods to family, friends, coworkers, or neighbors. A homemade cookie or cake represents time spent on behalf of the receiver, and time is a precious commodity these days. That's why it means so much when you make the effort to bake for a friend. Fresh baked goods say, "I care," in a way no store-bought treat can replicate.

The idea for this book came slowly. I am always looking for recipes that come together quickly and make a big impression. As a mother of four, a wife, an employee, a volunteer, a writer, and a friend, my days are spent running from baseball practice to the school, from band concerts to dance recitals, and everywhere in between. I need recipes that bring the refreshing tastes of home cooking to the dessert table without making a huge mess in the kitchen. With that idea in mind, *One Dirty Bowl* came to life.

I hope you love these recipes as much as I do. If you're looking to satisfy a brownie craving, try the Best-Ever Chocolate Fudge Lemon Brownies (p. 18)—they are hide-it-on-the-top-shelf good, but since the recipe makes enough for a 9 × 13 pan, there will be plenty to go around. If you're in the mood for something small and delightful, the Mini Pumpkin Oreos (p. 16) are the perfect bite-sized treat.

No matter why you're baking—be it to satisfy a craving or to impress your guests—you're sure to find a cookie, brownie, bar, cake, or sweet bread that will fill the order. And, because the recipes are quick and easy, you will be in and out of the kitchen in no time.

Happy baking!

Christina Dymock

Photo courtesy of Emily Penrod

Small & Scrumptious

Whether it's petits fours, cookies, candy pieces, or mini cupcakes, small desserts are all the rage. After a satisfying meal, it's nice to have a little taste of something sweet; it's like putting on just the right necklace to complement an outfit. When you make smaller-sized treats, it's possible to sample one of each without feeling as though you're wasting good food. Keep this in mind if you're serving a crowd since people are likely to sample everything.

Just because these desserts look delicate and there are a lot of them doesn't mean they have to take a lot of time. These sweet treats are easy to put together and are sure to satisfy.

Hazelnut Puffs

Makes 18

Ingredients

1 (8-oz.) pkg. frozen pastry puff dough

1 cup hazelnut spread

1 cup marshmallow crème

powdered sugar, for sprinkling

These little treats hardly take any time at all. They disappear quickly, so be sure to make enough. If you'd like something a little different, try substituting whipped cream for the marshmallow crème.

Thaw the pastry dough according to package directions. Once the dough is thawed, open it up and cut along each fold line. Then cut each section in half vertically. You should have 6 strips of dough. Now cut each of those strips into 6 squares.

Spray a cookie sheet lightly with nonstick cooking spray. Preheat the oven to 400 degrees or the temperature indicated on the package. Arrange the squares of dough on the cookie sheet so they aren't touching. Bake for 12–14 minutes or until light brown. Allow to cool.

Once the pastries are cool, divide the marshmallow crème among 18 squares. Repeat with the hazelnut spread. Use the remaining 18 puffs for the top of each treat. Sprinkle with powdered sugar and serve.

Mini Bundt Cakes with Pears

Makes 12

Ingredients

¾ cup sugar

2 Tbsp. oil

3 Tbsp. butter, softened

1 egg

½ tsp. vanilla

½ tsp. rum flavoring

1⅔ cups flour

1 tsp. baking powder

¼ tsp. baking soda

⅛ tsp. salt

1 tsp. cinnamon

½ cup buttermilk

1 cup diced fresh pears

These little cakes are dense and filled with pear and cinnamon flavors. The chopped pears provide a nice texture. The cakes are good warm or cold.

Preheat oven to 350 degrees. Grease and flour a mini bundt cake pan and set aside.

In a medium mixing bowl, combine the sugar, oil, butter, and egg. Add the vanilla, rum flavoring, flour, baking powder, baking soda, salt, cinnamon, and buttermilk. Use a wooden spoon to stir in the pears.

Divide the batter into the mini bundt cake slots and bake for 15–18 minutes, or until a toothpick inserted in the center comes out clean.

White Chocolate Cherry Delights

Makes 25

Ingredients

50 vanilla cookies

1 cup cherry-flavored frosting

1 (10-oz.) pkg. white chocolate-flavored candy coating

If you're looking to wow your friends for a party or just make movie night a little more special, these goodies will impress. You can change the frosting flavor to lemon, orange, or vanilla if you wish.

Place 25 vanilla cookies upside down on a cookie sheet. Using a decorator tip and bag (or a ziplock bag), pipe about 1 teaspoon of frosting onto the middle of each cookie. Top with the remaining cookies.

Melt the white chocolate–flavored coating according to package directions. While the candy coating is melting, lay a sheet of wax paper across your work surface. Once the candy coating is smooth, drop a cookie sandwich in and coat it with candy coating. Use a fork to remove the cookie sandwich, and place the delight on the wax paper to set. Repeat with the remaining cookies. Allow to set for 30 minutes before serving.

Raisin Pie Bites

Makes 24

Cooked raisins have a whole different appeal than eating a handful of dried fruit. When cooked, they plump up and the sugars become sweeter. When paired with brown sugar and walnuts, they make for the perfect bite of deep sweetness.

Ingredients

½ cup brown sugar

¼ cup sugar

½ tsp. cinnamon

2 Tbsp. dark corn syrup

½ cup raisins

2 (9-inch) frozen pie crusts, room temperature

¼ cup water

cinnamon sugar (optional)

Preheat the oven to 425 degrees. In a medium mixing bowl, stir together the brown sugar, sugar, and cinnamon. Add the dark corn syrup and raisins and stir until just combined. Set aside.

Unroll the pie crust. Use a round cookie cutter to cut out 4-inch circles. Place 1 tablespoon of raisin mixture on one half of the circle. Dip your finger in the water and then run it around the edge of the dough. The water will help the dough stick together. Fold the circle in half and seal the edges. Use a fork to poke holes in the top of the dough. Sprinkle with cinnamon sugar (optional).

Transfer to an ungreased cookie sheet and bake for 10–12 minutes, or until lightly browned. Once cooked, transfer it immediately to a wire rack to cool.

Cookie-Bottom Individual Cheesecakes

Makes 12

Ingredients

12 chewy chocolate chip cookies

1 (8-oz.) pkg. cream cheese, room temperature

4 Tbsp. sugar

1 egg

2 Tbsp. sour cream

1 tsp. vanilla

½ tsp. almond flavoring

vanilla frosting (optional)

mini chocolate chips for garnish (optional)

Cheesecake is one of those desserts that's rich enough to fill you up with a half of a slice. With these little beauties, you can eat the whole thing without worrying—they are just the right size.

Preheat the oven to 350 degrees. Line a muffin tin with cupcake liners. Drop 1 cookie into each cupcake liner. Set the pan aside.

In a medium mixing bowl, beat the cream cheese and sugar until light and fluffy, 3–5 minutes. Add the egg, sour cream, vanilla, and almond flavoring. Beat well, scraping down the sides as needed.

Divide the batter among the baking cups. Bake for 23–25 minutes or until a toothpick inserted in the center comes out clean.

Move the mini cheesecakes to a wire rack and allow to cool. Place them in the fridge for 3 hours before frosting, garnishing, or serving. Store extras in the fridge.

Ingredients

2¼ cups flour

1⅓ cups sugar

1 tsp. baking soda

1 tsp. salt

1¾ cups oil

¼ cup buttermilk

3 eggs

1 tsp. vanilla

2 large bananas

cream cheese frosting (12-oz.)

Banana Petits Fours

Makes 32

Perfect for any get-together, this recipe makes enough to serve a crowd. A quick way to dress them up for guests is to pipe a star on top and sprinkle with chopped nuts—walnuts or pecans would be best.

Preheat the oven to 350 degrees. Line a 10 × 15 jelly roll pan with aluminum foil. Spray with nonstick cooking spray and set aside.

In a large bowl, sift together the flour, sugar, baking soda, and salt. Add the oil, buttermilk, eggs, vanilla, and bananas. Beat well, scraping the sides of the bowl as you mix. Pour the batter into the prepared pan and bake for 27–30 minutes or until a toothpick inserted in the center comes out clean.

Allow to cool completely. Cut into small pieces and frost with cream cheese frosting. You can use a cookie cutter to create different shapes or simply a sharp knife for triangles and squares to make small sandwiches. If you're in a hurry, place a dollop of frosting in the center of the bottom piece of cake and press the top piece down to spread it to the edges. For a more finished look, use a #4B piping tip and frosting bag to pipe the frosting onto the cake.

Coconut Cups with Strawberry Filling

Makes 18

Ingredients

½ cup butter, room temperature

⅓ cup sugar

1 egg

1 tsp. coconut flavoring

1 tsp. vanilla

¼ tsp. salt

2¼ cups flour

½ cup coconut

½ cup white chocolate chips, chopped

1 (21-oz.) can strawberry pie filling

whipped cream, for topping

When you roll out the dough, you can make it a little thinner for more delicate cups, like waffle cones, and serve the dessert with a scoop of ice cream. Just be sure to reduce your cook time by two to three minutes so the cookies don't burn.

Cream together the butter and sugar in a medium mixing bowl. Add the egg and mix until light and fluffy. Add the coconut flavoring, vanilla, salt, and flour. Finally, add the coconut and chopped white chocolate chips. Form into a ball, wrap in plastic wrap, and place in the fridge for 1 hour.

After the dough has chilled, preheat the oven to 350 degrees.

Roll the dough out on a lightly floured surface. Use cookie cutters to make circles or squares. Bake in a muffin tin for 5–7 minutes or until the edges are light brown. Remove from oven and transfer to wire racks to cool.

Once cool, fill with strawberry filling and top with whipped cream to serve.

Roll-Over Cookie Bites

Makes 48

Sometimes getting different types of desserts to cook together is difficult. For example, cookies cook slowly, but caramels will burn fast. Balancing cookie dough and caramel can be tough. In these cookie bites, the caramel comes out soft but untainted while the cookie is crunchy on the outside and soft in the middle.

Ingredients

1 cup butter-flavored shortening

½ cup butter, room temperature

1½ cups sugar

½ cup brown sugar

2 eggs

1 tsp. vanilla

2 cups flour

¾ cup cocoa

1 tsp. baking soda

1 tsp. salt

1 (8-oz.) pkg. Rolos

Preheat the oven to 350 degrees. Spray a mini muffin tin with nonstick cooking spray and set aside.

Cream together the shortening, butter, sugar, and brown sugar in a medium bowl. Add the eggs one at a time, beating well after each addition. Next, add the vanilla, flour, cocoa, baking soda, and salt. Mix well.

Drop the batter by rounded teaspoonfuls into the prepared muffin tin. Add 1 Rolo to each muffin slot. Press it down far enough that the batter will mostly cover it but not so far that it touches the bottom of the pan. Bake for 20–25 minutes, or until the centers are set.

Ingredients

4 eggs

1 tsp. baking powder

½ tsp. salt

¾ cup sugar

1 tsp. vanilla

¾ cup flour

powdered sugar, for sprinkling

vanilla frosting

1 (12-oz.) tub chocolate frosting

slivered almonds (optional)

Little Chocolate Rolls

Makes 12

A few steps are involved in making a jelly roll cake, but none of them are especially hard. Since the cake bakes in less than fifteen minutes, it's one of the fastest-baked cakes around. You can also customize these cake rolls by changing out the filling, adding thin layers of different fruit spreads and frostings, or even filling it with ice cream.

Preheat the oven to 400 degrees. Line a 10 × 15 jelly roll pan with aluminum foil. Spray the foil with nonstick cooking spray and set aside.

In a medium bowl, beat the eggs, baking powder, and salt on high for 2 minutes. Slowly add the sugar and beat for 5 more minutes. Add the vanilla and flour and mix well. Pour the batter into the prepared pan and bake for 12–14 minutes or until the cake is set in the center and pulls away from the pan.

While the cake is cooking, lay a dish towel flat on the counter and sprinkle it with powdered sugar.

Remove the baked cake from the oven and allow it to cool for 3 minutes. Invert the cake onto the prepared towel and remove the aluminum foil. Cut ¼ inch off each side of the cake. Gently roll the cake, starting on one of the long sides and rolling the towel up with the cake. Allow to cool for 10 minutes.

Once the cake is cool, carefully unroll it. Frost it with vanilla frosting and roll it back up without the towel. Set the cake on a platter and place it in the fridge for 1 hour to set.

Once the cake is set, cut the roll into 12 pieces. Melt the chocolate frosting, 30 seconds on high in the microwave. Dip the top of each roll in the frosting. Roll it through the nuts if desired. Allow the frosting to set before serving.

Mini Pumpkin Oreos

Makes 30

Ingredients

- 1½ cups flour
- ½ tsp. baking soda
- ¼ tsp. baking powder
- ¼ tsp. salt
- 1 cup sugar
- 1 tsp. cinnamon
- ½ tsp. nutmeg
- ¼ tsp. ginger
- ½ cup butter, room temperature
- 1 egg
- ½ cup canned pumpkin
- caramel frosting

You may lament opening a can of pumpkin because you don't cook with it often enough to save the leftovers in the refrigerator. But there is a way to preserve the remaining pumpkin. Freezing it in a ziplock bag will allow you to cook more often with canned pumpkin without the guilt of throwing away half of the precious ingredient. Measure the pumpkin before putting it in the bag and label the bag with the amount and the date. When you're ready to use it, pull it out of the freezer at the same time you take out your butter to get it to room temperature, and it will be ready when you are.

Preheat the oven to 375 degrees. In a medium mixing bowl, whisk together the flour, baking soda, baking powder, salt, sugar, cinnamon, nutmeg, and ginger.

Add the butter, egg, and pumpkin and mix until well combined. Drop the batter by tablespoonfuls onto an ungreased cookie sheet.

Bake for 8–9 minutes, or until the cookies are set. Allow to cool for 1 minute on the cookie sheet before moving to a wire rack to finish cooling.

Once the cookies are cool, frost a cookie with the caramel frosting and then place another cookie on top. Repeat with the remaining cookies and frosting.

Beautiful Brownies & Bars

Brownies and bars are the epitome of easy desserts because you mix them in one bowl and bake them in one pan. To serve, be sure to cut them into easy-to-manage squares or rectangles. I once put the pan out before cutting and came back to find a huge square cut right out of the middle. Boys!

To achieve equal-sized pieces, use a kitchen ruler. Or cut the pan of brownies in half lengthwise and cut each half again, then twist the pan and do the same thing to make sixteen brownies. Since many of these recipes are rich, I cut each square again for thirty-two brownies or bars.

If you would like to remove the squares from the pan for serving, nestle each one in a cupcake liner. Hundreds of colors and designs are available, and presenting them this way will keep little fingers, or teenage fingers, from digging into the pan.

Best-Ever Chocolate Fudge Lemon Brownies

Makes 16

Ingredients

4 eggs

⅓ cup evaporated milk

½ cup butter, room temperature

2 cups sugar

¼ cup water

2 tsp. vanilla

1½ cups flour

⅓ cup cocoa

¼ tsp. salt

lemon frosting

chocolate fudge frosting

I can't say enough wonderful things about these brownies. I've served them to large groups of women, my family, and neighbors for a special treat. They are so delicious that it's hard not to eat more than your share. When you make them, beware: they are addictive.

Preheat the oven to 350 degrees. Spray a 9 × 13 baking pan with nonstick cooking spray and set aside.

In a medium mixing bowl, beat the eggs and evaporated milk until light and fluffy, 5 minutes on medium speed. Add the butter and sugar and beat well. Add the water, vanilla, flour, cocoa, and salt. Mix until the batter is smooth, scraping down the sides as needed.

Pour the batter into the prepared pan and bake for 30–32 minutes, or until a toothpick inserted in the center comes out clean. Place the pan on a wire rack and allow to cool for 2 hours. Frost with lemon frosting and let sit uncovered for 1–2 hours so the frosting can set. Frost with chocolate fudge frosting and serve.

In-the-Beginning Brownies

Makes 16

Ingredients

½ cup butter, room temperature

1 cup sugar

4 eggs

1 cup chocolate syrup

1 cup flour

2 Tbsp. cocoa

powdered sugar, for dusting

When a company comes up with a new product, like chocolate syrup, they hire professionals to create recipes that use their product to encourage home cooks to buy and use it. These brownies are akin to the chocolate syrup brownie recipes introduced by the makers of fine chocolate syrups.

Preheat the oven to 350 degrees. Spray a 9 × 13 baking pan with nonstick cooking spray and set aside.

Cream the butter and sugar in a medium mixing bowl. Add the eggs one at a time, beating well after each addition. Add the syrup, flour, and cocoa, and mix well. Bake for 30–35 minutes, or until a toothpick inserted in the center comes out clean. Allow to cool in the pan. Sprinkle with powdered sugar and serve.

Extreme Peanut Butter Bookies

Makes 32

Ingredients

1 (family-size) box brownie mix

eggs, oil, and water as indicated on the brownie mix box

½ cup creamy peanut butter

12 peanut butter cups

½ cup peanut butter baking chips

½ cup milk chocolate chips, divided

¼ cup mini peanut butter candy pieces, divided

1 (16-oz.) pkg. refrigerated peanut butter cookie dough

These bars are for the peanut butter and chocolate enthusiast in all of us. Part brownie, part cookie, and all parts scrumptious, these bars will have you falling head over heels.

Preheat the oven to 350 degrees. Spray a 9 × 13 baking pan with nonstick cooking spray and set aside.

In a medium mixing bowl, combine the brownie mix, eggs, oil, and water as indicated on the box to make the brownie batter. Pour the batter into the prepared pan.

Drop the creamy peanut butter by rounded tablespoonfuls into the brownie batter. Space your peanut butter cups evenly over the brownie batter and press down lightly. Then sprinkle the peanut butter chips, half the milk chocolate chips, and half the peanut butter candy pieces over the batter.

Next, break apart the squares of cookie dough. Smash each square between your palms to flatten it. Space the pieces of cookie dough evenly over the brownie batter. Sprinkle the remaining milk chocolate chips and peanut butter candy pieces over the top of the whole thing.

Bake for 45–60 minutes, or until a toothpick inserted in the center comes out with just a few crumbs. Allow to cool before serving, or serve warm with ice cream.

Variation:

Death-by-Chocolate Bookie:

Omit the peanut butter cookie dough, creamy peanut butter, peanut butter chips, and peanut butter candy pieces. Add refrigerated chocolate turtle cookie dough, ½ cup semisweet chocolate chips, ½ cup white chocolate chips, and 2 king-size chocolate bars broken into sections.

Mom's Butterscotch Bars

Makes 16 bars

Ingredients

½ cup butter

2 cups brown sugar

2 eggs

1 tsp. vanilla

2 tsp. baking powder

2 cups flour

¼ tsp. salt

maple or vanilla frosting (optional)

This recipe has always been a part of my life. I remember my mom making these for her annual Christmas party or to take to a church social. They were always a big hit. Mom frosted them with maple frosting, but I also enjoy them with vanilla or plain.

Preheat the oven to 350 degrees. Melt the butter in a medium microwave-safe mixing bowl. Stir in the brown sugar. Add the eggs one at a time, mixing well after each addition. Stir in the vanilla, baking powder, flour, and salt.

Spray a 9 × 13 cake pan with nonstick cooking spray. Scrape the batter into the pan and spread it to the edges. Bake for 20–22 minutes, or until a toothpick inserted in the center comes out clean. Serve alone or with maple or vanilla frosting.

No-Bake Peanut Butter Bars

Makes 32

These little babies come together in no time at all. If you're craving chocolate and peanut butter, this is the fastest way to meet that need. If you or your family is opposed to chopped nuts in desserts, you can use creamy peanut butter instead.

Ingredients

1 cup sugar

1 cup corn syrup

1 cup all-natural crunchy peanut butter

3 cups crispy rice cereal

1 (12-oz.) bag milk chocolate chips

Spray a 9 × 13 baking dish with nonstick cooking spray and set aside.

In a large saucepan over medium heat, bring the sugar and corn syrup to a boil. Remove from heat and stir in the peanut butter. Add the crispy rice cereal and stir to coat. Press the mixture into the prepared pan. Immediately sprinkle with chocolate chips. Once the chocolate chips have melted, use the back of a spoon to spread them out in an even layer.

To-Die-For Pecan Bars

Makes 16

Ingredients

1 (16.5-oz.) packet refrigerated snickerdoodle cookie dough (the flat sheet, not the roll)

½ cup cream

1½ cups brown sugar

½ cup butter

1½ tsp. vanilla

1½ cups powdered sugar

½ cup pecans

Using premade cookie dough takes all the stress out of these bars. You don't have to spread the dough because it will fill the pan as it cooks.

Preheat the oven to 350 degrees. Place the cookie dough, as a block, in an 8 × 8 baking dish and cook for 25–30 minutes or until the edges are slightly brown and a toothpick inserted in the center comes out clean. Set aside.

In a medium saucepan, stir together the cream and brown sugar. Cut the butter into 6 cubes and add to the cream mixture. Place the pan over medium heat and bring to a boil. Boil for 2½ minutes.

Take the pan off the burner and allow to cool for 5 minutes. Stir in the vanilla and powdered sugar until the mixture is smooth. Add the pecans and stir well. Pour the pecan topping over the cooled cookie dough. Place in the fridge to set—it will take about 1 hour. Cut and serve.

Variety S'mores Bars

Makes 16

Have you ever been to a party with a s'mores bar? The host will put out graham crackers, marshmallows, and a variety of chocolate bars so you can individualize your snacks. Then everyone at the party toasts their marshmallows over coals and assembles their s'mores. These cookies are a s'mores bar party in every bite. And with the assorted miniature candy bars, every square has a different combination of flavors.

Ingredients

1 (16.5-oz.) pkg. refrigerated sugar cookie dough (the flat sheet, not the roll)

1 (12-oz.) bag assorted miniature candy bars, unwrapped

16 marshmallows, cut in half

Preheat the oven to 350 degrees. Place the cookie dough, as a block, in an 8 × 8 inch baking dish. Cook for 25–30 minutes, or until the center is set and the edges are lightly browned.

Remove the pan from the oven and layer the miniature candy bars over the cookie. Don't leave space between candy bars. Cover the chocolate with a layer of marshmallows.

Turn the oven to low broil. Place the pan on the center rack and broil for 3–5 minutes, or until the marshmallows are lightly toasted. Remove the bars from the oven and allow to cool for 20 minutes before serving. (They will be messy but amazing.) Or allow them to set overnight for less chocolate-and-marshmallow gooeyness.

Chocolate Cream Cheese Strawberry Brownies

Makes 16 brownies

Ingredients

2¼ cups sugar, divided

½ cup shortening

4 eggs

2 cups flour

¼ cup special dark cocoa powder

½ cup cocoa powder

½ tsp. salt

½ cup evaporated milk

¼ cup water

2½ tsp. vanilla, divided

1 (8-oz.) pkg. cream cheese, room temperature

1 (21-oz.) can strawberry pie filling

Don't worry if your cream cheese mixture turns out a little chocolate looking; it all bakes up just fine. These are best made and eaten within two days because the strawberry topping tends to absorb into the brownie as time goes on. It's not a bad thing—it's just not as pretty.

Preheat the oven to 350 degrees. Spray a 9 × 13 baking pan with nonstick cooking spray and set aside.

In a large mixing bowl, cream 2 cups of sugar and the shortening. Add the eggs all at once and beat well. Add the flour, cocoa powders, salt, evaporated milk, water, and 2 teaspoons of vanilla. Mix until smooth, scraping down the sides as you go.

Pour the batter into the prepared pan. Use a rubber spatula to get as much of the batter out of the bowl as possible. Set the pan aside.

In that same bowl, beat the cream cheese, ½ teaspoon vanilla, and ¼ cup sugar until smooth. Drop by rounded tablespoonfuls into the brownie batter and use a knife to swirl the cream cheese mixture in with the brownie batter.

Open the strawberry pie filling and drop by rounded tablespoonfuls over the top of the brownie batter. Do not swirl in. Bake for 25–30 minutes or until a toothpick inserted in the center comes out clean. Allow to cool before serving.

Variation:

Raspberry Cream Cheese Brownies:

Replace the strawberry pie filling with raspberry pie filling.

Chocolate Cream Cheese Brownies:

Add 1 cup of semisweet chocolate chips to the brownie batter before pouring into the pan. Add 1½ tablespoons of cocoa powder to the cream cheese mixture. Omit the strawberry filling.

Very Vanilla Brownies

Makes 16

Ingredients

1½ cups flour

½ tsp. baking powder

½ tsp. salt

¾ cup butter, room temperature, cut into small pieces

1½ cups sugar

4 eggs

2 tsp. vanilla

½ tsp. almond extract

frosting (optional)

A friend of mine is allergic to chocolate. One rainy afternoon, I decided to take her brownies, and thus the vanilla brownie was born. You can use any flavor of frosting you'd like. I prefer a whipped frosting because it is a nice contrast to the dense brownie.

Preheat the oven to 350 degrees. Spray a 9 x 13 baking pan with nonstick cooking spray and set aside.

In a medium mixing bowl, sift together the flour, baking powder, and salt. Make a crater in the middle of the powdered ingredients and add the butter, sugar, eggs, vanilla, and almond extract. Mix until the batter is smooth, about 3 minutes. Pour into the prepared pan and bake for 25–30 minutes or until a toothpick inserted in the center comes out clean.

Frost with your choice of frosting, or simply sprinkle with powdered sugar, and serve.

Seriously Chunky Brownies

Makes 16

Ingredients

1½ cups semisweet chocolate chips, divided

½ cup butter

1 cup sugar

1¼ cups flour

2 eggs

1 tsp. vanilla

1 tsp. almond flavoring

2 Tbsp. cocoa

¾ cup quick oats

½ cup pecans

1 cup milk chocolate baking chunks

Thanks to the oats and a whole heap of chocolate, these brownies have a whole lot of heft, so I tend to cut them smaller than the average brownie. However, don't be afraid to go big if you're serving them as part of a brownie sundae.

Preheat the oven to 350 degrees. Spray a 9 × 13 baking pan with nonstick cooking spray and set aside.

In a medium-sized, microwave-safe mixing bowl, melt 1 cup of semisweet chocolate chips and the butter on half power in the microwave for 1 minute. Stir and repeat until the mixture is smooth and no chocolate chips remain.

Add the sugar and mix well. Add the flour, eggs, vanilla, almond flavoring, cocoa, and quick oats. Stir until the ingredients are incorporated, scraping down the sides as needed. Using a wooden spoon, stir in the pecans, chocolate baking chunks, and remaining semisweet chocolate chips. Pour into the prepared pan and bake for 35–40 minutes or until a toothpick inserted near the center comes out with large crumbs but no batter.

Sandwich Cookie Bars

Makes 16

Ingredients

1 Tbsp. butter

1 (11.5-oz.) bag milk chocolate chips

1 (14-oz.) can sweetened condensed milk

1 (14.3-oz.) pkg. chocolate sandwich cookies, roughly chopped

sprinkles (optional)

Prepare to go on cookie overload. These bars will be the hit of the day, and they are so easy to put together that you'll be making them all the time.

In a medium saucepan, melt together the butter and chocolate chips. Once the chocolate is smooth, remove the pan from the heat and stir in the sweetened condensed milk. Add the chopped cookies and stir lightly. You don't need to coat the cookies all the way; just make sure they are roughly incorporated. Spread the mixture into an 8 × 8 baking dish. (Garnish with sprinkles here if desired.) Use the back of a metal spoon to help press it into place. Allow to set for 1 hour before cutting.

Abracadabra Cookie Bars

Makes 24–36

When making these for in-house consumption, I toss on the toppings in the same order as I grab them off the shelf. When I make them to take somewhere, I do half the chips and coconut flakes and then layer the other half on top of that. It makes them look prettier. If you wait until they cool completely to cut them, they will cut with clean edges.

Ingredients

1 cup butter, softened

½ cup sugar

1 tsp. vanilla

2 cups flour

¼ tsp. salt

1 (14-oz.) can sweetened condensed milk

1 cup butterscotch chips

1 cup milk chocolate chips

½ cup sweetened coconut flakes

½ cup chopped pecans

Preheat the oven to 350 degrees. Spray a 9 × 13 baking pan with nonstick cooking spray and set aside.

Cream the butter and sugar in a medium mixing bowl. Add the vanilla, flour, and salt and mix until the batter is well combined and becomes crumbly. Use your fingers to press the batter into the prepared baking pan. Bake for 15 minutes.

Remove the pan from the oven and pour the sweetened condensed milk over the crust. Now, layer the butterscotch chips, chocolate chips, coconut flakes, and pecans over the top. You can do them in any order you like, or do half of each and then the other half again.

Bake for 25–30 minutes or until the edges are slightly brown. Do not overbake. Allow the bars to cool before serving.

Ingredients

¼ cup butter

1 cup chocolate chips

25 large marshmallows

4 cups crispy rice cereal

Chocolate Crispy Bars

Makes 9

Right before everything melts together in the pan, the chocolate is going to look pretty rough. Don't give up on it! Just keep stirring slowly, and it will all turn out okay.

Spray a 9 × 9 baking pan with nonstick cooking spray. Set aside.

Melt the butter in a large saucepan over low heat. Add the chocolate chips and marshmallows and stir well. Continue stirring until the marshmallows are melted and the mixture is smooth. Add the crispy rice cereal and stir to coat. Pour the mixture into the pan and spread it out evenly. You can spray your hands with nonstick cooking spray to press the mixture into the pan if needed. Allow to set before cutting.

Ingredients

¾ cup sugar

½ cup brown sugar

12 Tbsp. butter, room temperature

2 eggs

2 cups flour

½ cup unsweetened cocoa powder

1 tsp. baking soda

¼ tsp. salt

1 tsp. vanilla

1 king-size peanut butter Snickers bar

½ cup milk chocolate chips

Peanut Butter Goodness Bars

Makes 24

By adding the candy bar into the mix, you'll end up with pockets of sweet peanut butter within the cookie bars. It's a special moment to savor the flavor.

Preheat the oven to 350 degrees. Spray a 9 × 13 baking pan with nonstick cooking spray and set aside.

In a medium mixing bowl, cream the sugar, brown sugar, and butter until light and fluffy. Add the eggs and mix well. Add the flour, cocoa powder, baking soda, salt, and vanilla and mix until the batter is smooth. It will be thick like cookie batter.

Chop the candy bar into 24 equal pieces. Stir the candy bar and chocolate chips into the batter. Spread the batter into the prepared pan. Cook for 20–25 minutes or until set.

Ingredients

1 (16.5-oz.) box vanilla cake mix

1 cup creamy peanut butter

1 egg

¼ cup butter, melted

1 (14-oz.) can sweetened condensed milk

1 cup semisweet chocolate chips

Peanut Butter Love Bars

Makes 16

Do you love peanut butter, chocolate, and fudge? Well then hang on to your apron because you have found your perfect dessert. The deep peanut butter flavor is balanced with the sweet fudge and semisweet chocolate. These super-rich bars got their name because I always hear a lot of "I love yous" when a pan of these comes out of the oven. Share the love, baby. Share the love.

Preheat the oven to 350 degrees. Grease a 9 × 13 cake pan and set aside.

In a medium mixing bowl, beat together the cake mix, peanut butter, and egg. Reserve 1 cup of the mixture. Lightly press the rest of the peanut butter mixture into the prepared pan. This will make your crust. Bake for 10 minutes.

Now that your bowl is empty, add the butter, sweetened condensed milk, and semisweet chocolate chips. Mix until just combined. Pour this mixture over the top of the baked crust. Sprinkle the reserved peanut butter mixture over the chocolate chip mixture. Return the pan to the oven and bake for 20–25 minutes.

Over-the-Moon Brownies

Makes 16

If you're in the mood for a deep, thick, fudgy brownie, then this is your recipe. The cream cheese adds an extra layer of flavor that leaves you licking your fingers with happiness.

Ingredients

½ cup butter, room temperature

⅓ cup cocoa

1¼ cups sugar

1 (8-oz.) pkg. cream cheese, room temperature

1 tsp. vanilla

2 eggs

1 cup flour

¼ tsp. salt

½ cup walnuts, chopped

1 cup milk chocolate chips

Preheat the oven to 350 degrees. Spray a 9 x 13 baking pan with nonstick cooking spray and set aside.

In a medium mixing bowl, beat together the butter, cocoa, sugar, and cream cheese for 1 minute.

Add the vanilla and eggs and beat until combined. Scrape down the edges of the mixing bowl with a rubber spatula. Add the flour and salt. Finally, roughly mix in the walnuts and chocolate chips. Pour the batter into the prepared pan and spread the batter to the edges.

Bake for 30–35 minutes or until a toothpick inserted in the center comes out clean. Allow to cool for 15 minutes before serving.

Decadent Dessert Breads

Also called "quick breads," these luscious loaves are leavened with baking powder or baking soda, not with yeast like traditional breads. Quick breads can also include scones, biscuits, and muffins, though I've stuck to loaf pans in this section. That said, baking up one of these beauties doesn't require much—a bowl and a pan, and you're on your way.

To give or serve dessert bread, wrap it in a holiday kitchen towel and tie it with a ribbon, package it in parchment paper, place it in a bread bag, or cut it and arrange it on a decorative plate.

One of my favorite ways to serve sweet bread is to make frosting sandwiches. White Chocolate Pumpkin Bread (p. 44) with cream cheese frosting is a family favorite. Slice it thin and spread the frosting on thick. If you aren't serving right away, be sure to cover the bread to keep it moist.

Chocolate Chocolate Chip Bread

Makes 1 loaf

Ingredients

¼ cup oil

½ cup sugar

¼ cup brown sugar

2 eggs

1 tsp. vanilla

¼ cup sour cream

1 cup flour

½ tsp. salt

¾ tsp. baking soda

3 Tbsp. cocoa powder

½ cup mini chocolate chips

Can you really call it bread if it's full of chocolate? Um . . . yep! This recipe is best served warm, although a cold slice is nothing to turn your nose up at.

Preheat the oven to 350 degrees. Grease and flour a large loaf pan and set aside.

In a medium mixing bowl, beat the oil, sugar, brown sugar, and eggs for 3 minutes. Add the vanilla, sour cream, flour, salt, baking soda, and cocoa. Mix well. Pour the batter into the prepared pan and sprinkle with the mini chocolate chips. Bake for 50–55 minutes, or until a toothpick inserted in the center comes out clean.

Almond Bread

Makes 1 loaf

Ingredients

- ¾ cup butter, room temperature
- 4 oz. cream cheese, room temperature
- 1¼ cups sugar
- 2 Tbsp. honey
- 1 tsp. almond extract
- 1½ cups flour, divided
- 3 eggs
- ¼ cup slivered almonds

Almond flavoring has a sweet smell that sets it apart from other flavors; it's part nut and part sugar. When this bread is baking, your house is going to smell like a world-class bakery.

Preheat the oven to 325 degrees. Grease a large loaf pan and set aside.

In a medium mixing bowl, beat the butter and cream cheese until creamy. Add the sugar and beat until fluffy. Incorporate the honey and the almond extract into the batter. Add half the flour and mix. Add the eggs and then the other half of the flour, mixing well between additions.

Spoon the batter into the prepared loaf pan. Sprinkle the nuts over the top of the batter. Bake for 50–55 minutes, or until a toothpick inserted in the center comes out clean and the top is golden brown. Do not underbake or the bread will fall. When the bread is done, run a knife around the edge of the pan and then allow the bread to cool for 15 minutes before removing it from the pan and placing it on a wire rack to finish cooling.

Lemon Bread with Blueberry Streusel

Makes 1 loaf

The contrast between the lemon bread and blueberry streusel makes this one of the most beautiful breads in the world. It looks good on a plate, through the glass of a cake keeper, or lying on a napkin. And since it tastes as good as it looks, you're going to love it.

Ingredients

½ cup sugar

¼ cup butter

2 eggs

½ cup milk

1 cup flour

1 tsp. vanilla

1 tsp. lemon flavoring

1 Tbsp. freshly grated lemon rind

1 tsp. baking powder

¼ tsp. salt

For streusel:

½ Tbsp. butter, room temperature

¼ cup quick oats

2 Tbsp. sugar

1 Tbsp. brown sugar

1 Tbsp. flour

½ cup blueberries

Preheat the oven to 350 degrees. Spray a medium loaf pan with nonstick cooking spray and set aside.

In a medium mixing bowl, beat together the sugar, butter, and eggs until smooth. Add the milk, flour, vanilla, lemon flavoring, lemon rind, baking powder, and salt. Mix well. Pour the batter into the prepared pan. Use a rubber spatula to scrape out the bowl.

Once the bowl is scraped out, add all the streusel ingredients except the blueberries to the bowl. Beat until well combined. Stir in the blueberries. Sprinkle the mixture over the batter in the loaf pan, but do not stir it in. Bake for 45–50 minutes or until a toothpick inserted in the center comes out clean.

White Chocolate Pumpkin Bread

Makes 24 servings or 2 loaves

Ingredients

1 (15-oz.) can pumpkin puree

3¼ cups flour

4 tsp. baking powder

1 tsp. salt

1½ tsp. cinnamon

½ tsp. nutmeg

½ tsp. ginger

1 cup milk

½ cup oil

½ cup brown sugar

1 tsp. vanilla

1 cup white chocolate chips

1 cup Craisins

1 cup chopped walnuts

Pumpkin bread is traditionally served in the fall, but feel free to break tradition and give this bread a try any time of year. It makes a wonderful gift for neighbors or friends. Just remember to grease your bread pans well so that the bread slides out in one piece.

Preheat the oven to 350 degrees. Grease and flour 2 large loaf pans and set aside.

In a large mixing bowl, combine the pumpkin, flour, baking powder, salt, cinnamon, nutmeg, ginger, and milk. Add the oil, brown sugar, and vanilla. Stir until the batter is smooth but not whipped. Add the white chocolate chips, Craisins, and walnuts and pour into the prepared pans.

Bake for 50–55 minutes or until a toothpick inserted in the center comes out clean. Allow to cool in the pans for 5 minutes. Run a butter knife between the bread and the pans to loosen the bread. Transfer the bread to wire racks to finish cooling.

Carrot Bread

Makes 12 servings

Ingredients

½ cup sugar

½ cup oil

⅔ cup flour

2 eggs

¾ tsp. cinnamon

⅛ tsp. allspice

½ tsp. baking soda

1 tsp. vanilla

¼ tsp. salt

1 cup shredded carrots

1 cup nuts, plus more (optional)

cream cheese frosting (optional)

Fans of carrot cake will love this bread. I'm a fan of any recipe that includes a vegetable and makes it taste this good. And what would carrot cake or carrot bread be without a little cream cheese frosting? While the recipe can hold its own, there's nothing wrong with a little embellishment.

Preheat the oven to 350 degrees. Grease a medium loaf pan and set aside.

In a medium mixing bowl, stir together the sugar, oil, flour, eggs, cinnamon, allspice, baking soda, vanilla, and salt until smooth. Add the carrots. Add the nuts if desired. Pour batter into prepared pan.

Bake for 40 minutes, or until a toothpick inserted in the center comes out clean. Allow the loaf to cool for 5–10 minutes before transferring to a wire rack to cool completely. If desired, frost with cream cheese frosting and sprinkle with additional nuts.

Orange Bread

Makes 12 servings

This thick bread carries its weight in flavor. The cream cheese brings something tangy to the sweetness of the orange flavoring.

Ingredients

4 oz. cream cheese, room temperature

¼ cup shortening

¾ cup sugar

1 egg

1¼ cups flour

1 tsp. salt

2 tsp. baking powder

1 tsp. vanilla

¼ cup milk

½ cup orange juice

2 Tbsp. additional orange juice (optional)

Preheat the oven to 375 degrees. Grease a large loaf pan and set aside.

Cream together the cream cheese, shortening, and sugar until light and fluffy. Add the egg and mix well. Add the flour, salt, baking powder, vanilla, milk, and orange juice.

Spoon batter into prepared loaf pan and bake for 55 minutes, or until a toothpick inserted in the center comes out clean. Let the loaf cool in the pan for 10 minutes. Run a knife around the edge of the pan to loosen the bread before transferring it to a wire rack to finish cooling. Brush with remaining orange juice if desired.

Butter Rum Bread

Makes 12 servings

Ingredients

2¼ cups flour

1 cup brown sugar

2 tsp. baking powder

½ tsp. baking soda

½ tsp. salt

½ tsp. vanilla

1 tsp. rum flavoring

1 egg

1 cup buttermilk

2 Tbsp. butter, melted

½ cup chopped pecans

Just like any sweet bread, this loaf comes out dense and delicious. If necessary, the pecans on top can be left off. But if you're a big pecan lover, feel free to mix an extra half cup of chopped pecans into the batter. When I introduced my family to this recipe, they went bonkers. The poor loaf didn't stand a chance against four hungry kidlets. When you make this sweet bread, be sure to take evasive measures—like hiding a slice in the pantry behind the oatmeal.

Preheat the oven to 350 degrees. Spray a large loaf pan with nonstick cooking spray. Set aside.

In a medium mixing bowl, combine the flour, brown sugar, baking powder, baking soda, and salt. Add the vanilla, rum flavoring, egg, buttermilk, and butter. Beat with a hand mixer just until the batter is smooth. Pour the batter into the prepared loaf pan. Sprinkle the chopped pecans on top of the bread. Bake for 45–50 minutes, or until a toothpick inserted in the center comes out clean.

Enticing Cookies

The name "cookie" comes from the Dutch word *koekje*, which means "little cake." While a cake is made from thin batter (often thinned with water or milk), cookies use butter or oil as their binding agent. This makes them dense enough to hold their shape as dough.

The first cookies were what we would consider wafers. They were thin, crisp, and only lightly sweetened. Today, cookies come in all shapes and sizes. They can be cooked to a crisp or made soft and chewy. They can also include all types of ingredients, from chocolate to bacon. In the following pages, you're sure to find a cookie recipe that calls to you.

Coconut Macaroons

Makes 24

Ingredients

1½ cups flaked coconut

⅓ cup sugar

2 Tbsp. flour

⅛ tsp. salt

2 egg whites

1 tsp. vanilla

½ tsp. rum extract

These cookies are delicious on their own. However, if you want to step these up a notch, try dipping them in chocolate. Or, if you're looking for a really amazing dessert, place three tablespoons of hot fudge sauce in the bottom of a small bowl, add two or three coconut macaroons, and then cover with a tablespoon of caramel sauce. Microwave for twenty to thirty seconds and serve.

Preheat the oven to 325 degrees. In a medium mixing bowl, combine the coconut, sugar, flour, and salt.

Add the egg whites, vanilla, and rum extract. Stir until well combined.

Use a teaspoon to measure out cookie balls, and place the balls onto a greased cookie sheet. Bake for 18–20 minutes, or until the edges are golden brown and the cookies are set.

Ingredients

9 marshmallows

1 cup butter-flavored shortening

1 cup sugar

½ cup brown sugar

⅔ cup cocoa

2 cups flour

1 tsp. baking soda

½ tsp. salt

2 eggs

1 tsp. vanilla

sugar, for sprinkling (optional)

Marshmallow-in-the-Middle Cookies

Makes 36

This recipe came to me through a dear friend. After I tasted the cookies, she became an even better friend. The key is to make sure the marshmallows are good and frozen. You can cut them and freeze them up to a day before making the cookies.

Preheat the oven to 400 degrees. Cut the marshmallows into fourths and place in the freezer while you make the cookie dough.

Cream the shortening and sugars together in a medium mixing bowl. Add the cocoa, flour, baking soda, salt, eggs, and vanilla, and mix well. The batter will be thick like sugar cookie dough.

Remove the marshmallows from the freezer. Use a tablespoon to scoop out some batter. Wrap the batter around the frozen marshmallow, making sure there are no cracks. If desired, sprinkle with sugar just before baking. Place cookie balls on an ungreased cookie sheet and bake for 5 minutes. Allow to cool on the baking sheet for 1 minute before moving them to a wire rack.

Lemon Spritz Cookies

Makes 45

Sometimes, having the right tool can be all it takes to make something look fancy. A cookie press is one of those tools. These cookies can be made into balls and baked, or the batter can be put through a cookie press to make delicate shapes.

Ingredients

2 cups butter, room temperature

1 cup sugar

1 egg

1 tsp. vanilla

1 tsp. lemon flavoring

1 Tbsp. lemon juice

3 drops yellow food coloring

4 cups flour

Preheat the oven to 375 degrees. In a large mixing bowl, beat the butter and sugar until light and fluffy. Add the egg, vanilla, lemon flavoring, lemon juice, food coloring, and flour. Mix until the batter is smooth.

Use a cookie press to make shaped cookies, or simply spoon out the batter by teaspoonfuls and place it on an ungreased cookie sheet. Bake for 10 minutes or until edges are set. Allow to cool for 1 minute on cookie sheet before moving to a wire rack. Store in a cool, dry place.

Snap-and-Crackle Cookies

Makes 45

Ingredients

1 cup butter, room temperature

1 cup brown sugar

1 cup sugar

2 eggs

2 tsp. vanilla

1½ cups flour

1 tsp. baking powder

1 tsp. baking soda

2 cups oatmeal

1 cup shredded coconut

2 cups crispy rice cereal

These wonderful cookies turn out thin. They have a delicious flavor, and the cereal adds a little of the unexpected.

Preheat the oven to 350 degrees. Cream the butter and sugars in a large mixing bowl. Add the eggs and vanilla and beat until fluffy. Mix in the flour, baking powder, baking soda, oatmeal, coconut, and cereal.

Drop batter by tablespoonfuls onto an ungreased cookie sheet. Bake for 10–12 minutes or until set.

Ingredients

½ cup shortening

1 cup brown sugar

1 egg

¼ cup milk

1¼ cups flour

1 cup oats

½ tsp. baking soda

1 tsp. baking powder

1 tsp. salt

½ tsp. nutmeg

1 tsp. cinnamon

1½ cups raisins

½ cup nuts of your choice, chopped (optional)

Old-Fashioned Oatmeal Raisin Cookies

Makes 36

Do you remember the smell of oatmeal cookies when you'd walk through the door after a day of spelling tests and recess? I won't try to tell you that eating cookies is good for your health, but you can't go wrong with oats, raisins, and nuts when they taste this good together.

Preheat the oven to 375 degrees. In a medium mixing bowl, cream the shortening and brown sugar. Add the egg and beat well. Incorporate the milk. Then add the flour, oats, baking soda, baking powder, salt, nutmeg, and cinnamon and mix until well combined. Stir in the raisins. If desired, you can stir in the nuts at this time.

Drop batter by rounded teaspoonfuls onto an ungreased cookie sheet. Bake for 8–10 minutes or until centers are set and edges are delicately browned.

Nutty Cookies

Makes 24

Don't be fooled by the ease of preparation—these cookies are full of wonderful butter and nut flavors.

Ingredients

1 cup butter

½ cup powdered sugar

2 cups flour

½ tsp. salt

1 tsp. vanilla

1 cup chopped nuts of your choice (optional)

Cream together the butter and powdered sugar. Add the flour, salt, and vanilla. The batter will get thick and sticky. Transfer the dough to a piece of plastic wrap. Wrap up well while forming the dough into a log shape, 2–3 inches around and 10 inches long. Refrigerate for 3–4 hours.

Preheat the oven to 350 degrees.

Slice the log into ¼-inch-thick slices. Place the slices on an ungreased cookie sheet. Bake for 10–15 minutes, or until set and the edges are delicately browned. Transfer to a wire rack to cool.

Banana Cookies

Makes 36

Ingredients

2 large bananas, peeled

⅔ cup shortening

2 eggs

1 cup sugar

2¼ cups flour

2 tsp. baking powder

¼ tsp. baking soda

1 tsp. salt

1 tsp. vanilla

1 cup chocolate chips (optional)

1 cup crushed nuts (optional)

The older your bananas, the darker these cookies will turn out. If the stem still has a little green, then you'll get a sharp-flavored cookie. If the bananas have aged, the flavor will be mellow. You can choose any kind of nuts and either semisweet or milk chocolate chips—or you can leave them all out for a smooth, cake-like cookie.

Preheat the oven to 350 degrees. In a large bowl, use a hand mixer to crush the bananas. Add the shortening and eggs and beat until smooth. Add the sugar, flour, baking powder, baking soda, salt, and vanilla, and mix well. If desired, stir in the chocolate chips and walnuts with a wooden spoon.

Drop batter by tablespoonfuls onto ungreased cookie sheets, leaving about 2 inches between cookies. Bake for 8–10 minutes, or until the centers are set and the edges are lightly browned.

Ingredients

2 egg whites

1/8 tsp. salt

1/8 tsp. cream of tartar

½ tsp. raspberry flavoring

2 drops red food coloring

½ cup sugar

Raspberry Meringue Cookies

Makes 30

While piping the cookies will give you a uniform look, you can also just spoon them onto the cookie sheet. Use two spoons, one to scoop out the mixture and the back of the other spoon to push it onto the cookie sheet.

Preheat the oven to 225 degrees. In a medium mixing bowl, beat the egg whites, salt, and cream of tartar until soft peaks form, about 5 minutes. Pour the raspberry flavoring and food coloring over the sugar in the measuring cup. Slowly add the sugar mixture to the egg mixture. Beat together until stiff peaks form.

Spoon by heaping teaspoonfuls onto an ungreased, light-colored cookie sheet. Bake for 1½ hours. Turn off the oven and open the oven door. Once the oven has cooled, remove the cookie sheet and store the cookies in a cool, dry place.

Elvis's Kisses

Makes 24

Ingredients

- ¾ cup brown sugar
- ⅓ cup peanut butter
- ¼ cup butter-flavored shortening
- 1½ Tbsp. milk
- 1 tsp. vanilla
- 1 egg
- 1 ripe banana, medium-sized
- 1 cup flour
- ½ tsp. baking soda
- ¼ tsp. salt
- ½ cup peanuts
- ½ cup milk chocolate chips

It's well known that Elvis loved peanut butter and banana sandwiches, so I imagine he would have loved these cookies too.

Preheat the oven to 350 degrees. Spray a mini muffin tin with nonstick cooking spray and set aside.

Cream together the brown sugar, peanut butter, and shortening in a medium mixing bowl. Add the milk, vanilla, egg, and banana and mix well, scraping down the sides of the bowl as needed. Add the flour, baking soda, and salt.

Divide the batter into the mini muffin pan. Sprinkle the peanuts and chocolate chips evenly over the batter in each cup. Bake for 8–10 minutes, or until set. Transfer to a wire rack for cooling.

Paper Bag Cookies

Makes 24

Ingredients

2 Tbsp. cinnamon

½ cup + 2 Tbsp. sugar, divided

9 oz. cream cheese, room temperature

1 cup butter, room temperature

2 eggs

2 cups flour

2 tsp. baking powder

¼ tsp. salt

The paper bag technique can be used for coating any number of desserts: powdered sugar donuts, chocolate crinkle cookies, and, of course, these wonderful cinnamon-sugar cookies.

Preheat the oven to 375 degrees. Pour the cinnamon and ½ cup of sugar into a paper lunch sack. Set aside.

In a medium mixing bowl, cream together the cream cheese and butter until smooth. Add the eggs one at a time, mixing well after each addition. Add the flour, baking powder, 2 tablespoons of sugar, and the salt. Drop by rounded teaspoonfuls onto an ungreased cookie sheet and bake for 12–15 minutes, or until set.

While the cookies are still warm, place 3–4 cookies in the paper sack. Fold the top over and shake gently to coat the cookies with the cinnamon and sugar. Place the cookies on a wire rack to cool. Repeat with all cookies.

Dark Chocolate and Caramel Cookies

Makes 24

Ingredients

2½ cups flour

¾ cup cocoa (use a cocoa with a darker blend, such as Hershey's special dark cocoa powder)

1 tsp. baking soda

1 cup sugar

1 cup brown sugar

1 cup butter, room temperature

2 tsp. vanilla

2 eggs

½ cup white chocolate chips

12 soft caramel candies, unwrapped and chopped into fourths

If you want to add just one more level of decadence to these already amazing cookies, sprinkle a few pieces of sea salt on the top right after you take them out of the oven. It looks beautiful, and the salt, caramel, and chocolate in one bite creates a flavor you can't resist.

Preheat the oven to 350 degrees. In a medium mixing bowl, whisk together the flour, cocoa, baking soda, sugar, and brown sugar. Make a crater in the middle of the mixture, and place the butter, vanilla, and eggs inside. Using a hand mixer, combine the ingredients. Add the white chocolate chips and chopped caramels.

Measure out teaspoons of dough and roll into balls. Place the balls on an ungreased cookie sheet. Make sure the caramel doesn't touch the cookie sheet or it will cook too fast. Bake for 8–10 minutes.

Bud Cookies

Makes 24

Ingredients

½ cup butter, room temperature

¼ cup butter-flavored shortening

½ cup sugar

½ cup brown sugar

2 eggs

1 tsp. vanilla

1 tsp. baking soda

½ tsp. salt

2¼ cups flour

1 (3.4-oz.) box vanilla pudding

¾ cup white chocolate chips

½ cup Craisins

½ cup walnuts

You've probably made cookie recipes before and wondered why your cookies don't look like the ones in the picture. One way to get photo-quality cookies is to put some of the mix-ins, like chocolate chips, on top of the ball of cookie dough. When the cookies bake, some of the ingredients will be on the top of the cookie. They'll look prettier, and it doesn't take much effort at all.

Preheat the oven to 350 degrees. In a medium mixing bowl, cream together the butter, shortening, sugar, and brown sugar. Add the eggs and beat until fluffy. Add the vanilla, baking soda, salt, flour, and vanilla pudding. Mix until a thick dough forms.

Add the white chocolate chips, Craisins, and nuts. Use a wooden spoon to roughly incorporate them into the dough.

Drop the dough by tablespoonfuls onto an ungreased cookie sheet. Bake for 9–11 minutes, or until cookies are set.

Ginger Softies

Makes 32

Light and delicious, Ginger Softies are the perfect combination of sugar cookies and ginger snaps. Traditional ginger snaps are shaped into balls and then rolled in sugar. By using sugar instead of flour to roll out the dough, you save a step in the preparation process.

Ingredients

½ cup butter, softened

½ cup sugar

1 egg

½ cup molasses

½ cup sour cream

1 tsp. baking soda

½ tsp. cinnamon

½ tsp. ginger

¼ tsp. salt

¼ tsp. nutmeg

3⅓ cups flour

sugar, for rolling dough

cream cheese frosting (optional)

Preheat the oven to 375 degrees. In a medium mixing bowl, cream the butter and sugar. Add the egg and mix well. Add the molasses, sour cream, baking soda, cinnamon, ginger, salt, and nutmeg. Stir until all the spices are well incorporated. Add the flour and mix until combined.

Sprinkle sugar over the counter as you would flour. Roll the dough out to ¼-inch thickness. Cut the dough with cookie cutters or use a knife to cut into quarter-sized pieces. Place the cookies on an ungreased cookie sheet. Bake for 6–8 minutes, or until the edges of the cookies are set. Transfer to a wire rack to cool. If desired, frost with cream cheese frosting.

Chocolate Graham Cracker Cookies

Makes 36

As far as cookies go, these guys are the cat's meow!

Ingredients

¾ cup butter, room temperature

½ cup sugar

½ cup brown sugar

1 cup graham cracker crumbs (8 crackers)

⅓ cup cocoa

1¼ cups flour

½ tsp. baking soda

1 tsp. salt

1 egg

1 tsp. vanilla

Preheat the oven to 350 degrees. In a medium mixing bowl, cream the butter and sugars until light and fluffy, about 5 minutes. Add the graham cracker crumbs, cocoa, flour, baking soda, salt, egg, and vanilla. Mix well. Drop by rounded spoonfuls onto an ungreased cookie sheet. Bake for 9–11 minutes, or until set.

Santa's Favorite Cookies

Makes 24

Ingredients

1 cup butter, room temperature

¾ cup sugar

¾ cup brown sugar

2 eggs

1 tsp. vanilla

2¼ cups flour

⅓ cup dark cocoa powder

½ tsp. salt

1 (11.5-oz.) pkg. semisweet chocolate chips

1 chocolate bar, for shavings

marshmallow or vanilla frosting

For most of the year, I make these with shredded chocolate. But on Christmas Eve, our family crushes candy canes to sprinkle on top for Santa.

Preheat the oven to 375 degrees. In a medium mixing bowl, cream together the butter, sugar, and brown sugar with a hand mixer. Add the eggs and vanilla and mix well.

Next, add the flour, cocoa, and salt. Mix until the dough is a dark chocolate color. Add the chocolate chips, and stir them in with a wooden spoon. Drop dough by rounded tablespoonfuls onto an ungreased cookie sheet. Bake for 8–10 minutes, or until set. Transfer to a wire rack and allow to cool.

Use a cheese grater to make chocolate shavings out of the candy bar. Once the cookies have cooled, frost with marshmallow or vanilla frosting. Sprinkle the chocolate shavings over the cookies.

Brownie Mallow Cookies

Makes 24

Ingredients

¾ cup sugar

¼ cup brown sugar

2 eggs

½ cup cocoa

3 Tbsp. butter, room temperature

¼ tsp. baking powder

¾ cup flour

½ tsp. salt

1 tsp. vanilla

12 chocolate brownie marshmallows (optional)

These brownie cookies are deep in flavor and texture. They taste and feel like you're biting into a fudgy brownie. I like to serve them as cookie sandwiches with a chocolate marshmallow middle, but you can easily serve them on their own, or simply frosted and sprinkled, to get the same wow factor.

Preheat the oven to 350 degrees. Beat the sugar, brown sugar, and eggs until light and fluffy, about 4 minutes. Add the cocoa and butter and beat until well combined. Add the baking powder, flour, salt, and vanilla and mix well.

Drop batter by tablespoonfuls onto an ungreased cookie sheet or roll into balls. Bake for 8–10 minutes, or until the centers are set.

If desired, place 1 marshmallow on top of the first half of the cookies and return the pan to the oven for 3 minutes. Top with the remaining cookies to make cookie sandwiches.

3X Chocolate Cookies

Makes 24

Ingredients

¼ cup butter, room temperature

¼ cup butter-flavored shortening

½ cup granulated sugar

½ cup brown sugar

1 egg

1 tsp. vanilla

1½ cups flour

¼ cup cocoa powder

½ tsp. baking soda

½ tsp. baking powder

½ tsp. salt

¾ cup semisweet chocolate chips

¾ cup white chocolate chips

It's a bit harder to tell when chocolate cookies are done than when regular chocolate chip cookies are. One test is to take the pan out of the oven and smack it against the counter. If the cookies deflate, they are ready to come out. If they stay puffy, they need a minute or two more.

Preheat the oven to 350 degrees. In a large mixing bowl, cream together the butter, shortening, sugar, and brown sugar. Add the egg and vanilla and beat until fluffy. Add the flour, cocoa powder, baking soda, baking powder, and salt. Mix until well combined. Sprinkle in both types of chocolate chips.

Drop the dough by rounded tablespoonfuls onto an ungreased cookie sheet. Bake for 8–11 minutes, or until cookies are set.

Ingredients

½ cup butter, softened

1½ cups sugar

2 eggs

1 tsp. vanilla

½ tsp. baking soda

½ tsp. baking powder

½ tsp. salt

1 cup pumpkin

2 tsp. cinnamon

½ tsp. allspice

½ tsp. nutmeg

½ cup sour cream

5 cups flour, plus more for dusting

cream cheese frosting, sprinkles, and other decorations

Pumpkin Sugar Cookies

Makes 24–30

Pumpkin cookies are traditionally cake-like. However, these cookies can be cut out with cookie cutters and retain their shape when baked. It's a nice change to have the pumpkin-flavored cookies in the fall and save the traditional sugar cookies for other times of the year.

Cream together the butter and sugar. Add the eggs and vanilla and beat well. Add the baking soda, baking powder, salt, pumpkin, cinnamon, allspice, nutmeg, and sour cream. Beat until smooth. Add the flour 1 cup at a time until the dough is thick and smooth. It will be sticky, but it should not be runny.

Divide the dough into 2 equal portions. Wrap the portions in plastic wrap and chill in the fridge overnight. This is an important step because it allows the flavors to mature and the dough to firm up for rolling.

Preheat the oven to 425 degrees.

Lightly dust the counter with flour and coat your rolling pin. Leave half of the dough in the fridge while you work with the other half. Roll the dough into a ¼-inch-thick rectangle. Cut out with cookie cutters. Place cookie dough cutouts on cookie sheets. Repeat with remaining half of cookie dough. Bake for 10–15 minutes, or until cookies are cooked through. Remove cookies from the cookie sheet to wire racks to cool. Once cool, frost with cream cheese frosting and decorate.

Divine Sweets

For over four decades, my family has been making candy for the holidays. Growing up with one day of the year (the day after Thanksgiving) dedicated to chocolate dipping was like having my own golden ticket.

Don't worry—for these yummy sweets, you won't need to temper chocolate or whip fondant by hand. The recipes are all easy and still meet my high standards. A particular favorite in our family is the Peanut Butter Truffle Bars (p. 78). They melt across your tongue and are much easier than other versions I've tried. I've also developed several variations of the recipe for different family members' preferences.

Because these recipes are so easy, there's no reason to relegate them to once-a-year baking. You can try something new once a month or make favorites for birthdays or to celebrate accomplishments.

Rocky Road

Makes 16 servings

Ingredients

2 cups semisweet chocolate chips

½ cup butter

½ tsp. salt

4 cups mini marshmallows

1 cup roughly chopped walnuts

Rocky Road is one of those traditional flavors that feels like it's been around since the beginning of time. However, the combination of chocolate, marshmallows, and nuts in ice cream started in the late 1920s. The original combination had walnuts, but almonds are now the mainstay. For this recipe, I went old school and pulled out the walnuts, but feel free to change it up if you'd like.

Prepare a loaf pan by lining it with plastic wrap. Make sure the wrap reaches each corner. Set aside.

Melt the chocolate chips and butter over low heat. Stir constantly until the chocolate is smooth. Remove from heat and allow to cool for 5 minutes. Add the salt, marshmallows, and walnuts. Stir until everything is evenly covered in chocolate. Pour the chocolate into the prepared loaf pan.

Place the loaf pan in the fridge for 2 hours to set. To serve, remove the loaf from the pan, unwrap the chocolate, and slice as you would a loaf of bread.

Rum Balls

Makes 24

Perfect for when you're in a hurry and want to pull out a show stopper, these rum balls look beautiful placed in candy cups for serving. If you're feeling ambitious, you can refrigerate the fondant, dip it in chocolate, and then roll it in the nuts. When dipped in chocolate, they will store for up to a month and don't need to be refrigerated.

Ingredients

5–5¼ cups powdered sugar, divided

4 oz. cream cheese, softened

2 Tbsp. evaporated milk

1 tsp. rum flavoring

1 tsp. vanilla

1 cup crushed almonds

Combine 4½ cups powdered sugar, cream cheese, evaporated milk, rum flavoring, and vanilla in a large mixing bowl until creamy. Slowly add powdered sugar until the batter turns into a thick paste. You may not need all the powdered sugar. Scrape the sides as needed. Cover with plastic wrap and place in the fridge for 2 hours.

Pour the nuts onto a plate. Once the batter is chilled, use a spoon to scrape out about 1½ teaspoons of batter. Dust your hands with powdered sugar and roll the batter into a ball. Then roll the ball in the nuts to cover it. Place the ball on a piece of wax paper or in a paper candy cup. Repeat steps with remaining batter.

Stores for up to 4 days if covered with plastic wrap and kept in the refrigerator.

Ingredients

½ cup Reese's mini pieces

¼ cup butter

½ cup milk chocolate chips

½ cup peanut butter baking chips

Peanut Butter Truffle Bars

Makes 12

Be prepared to fall in love. These bars are melt-in-your-mouth marvelous. When stored in an airtight container, they will hold their shape and flavor for up to two weeks, but they'll never wait around that long. You can also dip them in chocolate to make truffle candy bars like the ones sold in specialty chocolate shops. These bars are so elegant that no one will ever have to know how quickly you threw them together.

Divide the mini peanut butter candy pieces among 12 slots in a candy bar mold. Set aside. Place the butter, milk chocolate chips, and peanut butter baking chips in a small saucepan over low heat. Stir occasionally until the chocolate is smooth. Pour chocolate into molds and allow to set.

Variations:

Milk Chocolate Truffles: Omit the peanut butter candy pieces and peanut butter chips and increase the milk chocolate chips to 1 cup.

Mint Chocolate Truffles: Omit the peanut butter candy pieces and peanut butter chips, increase the milk chocolate chips to 1 cup, and add ½ teaspoon of mint flavoring.

Almond Chocolate Truffles: Omit the peanut butter candy pieces and peanut butter chips, increase the milk chocolate chips to 1 cup, and add ½ teaspoon of almond flavoring and ¼ cup of chopped almonds.

Dark Chocolate Truffles: Omit the candy pieces and peanut butter chips, and instead of milk chocolate chips use 1 cup of semisweet chocolate chips.

Hazelnut Ice Cream Topping

Makes 16 servings

Hazelnut spread has made its way into the hearts and pantries of millions of people across the country. They like it plain, they like it as a dip, and they love it mixed into their desserts. Ice cream sundaes are no exception, and this topping is sure to give you and your family your hazelnut fix.

Ingredients

2 cups sugar

1 cup evaporated milk

3 Tbsp. butter

1 cup hazelnut spread

1 (7-oz.) tub marshmallow cream

1 tsp. vanilla

Over medium-high heat, bring the sugar, evaporated milk, and butter to a boil in a medium saucepan. Boil for 3 minutes. Remove the pan from the stove and add the hazelnut spread, marshmallow cream, and vanilla. Beat with a hand mixer for 3–5 minutes, or until ultra-smooth. Store in the fridge for up to 10 days.

Honey Caramels

Makes 72

Ingredients

2 cups sugar

1 cup honey

1 cup corn syrup

½ cup butter, plus more for the pan

1⅔ cups evaporated milk

1 tsp. vanilla

You can definitely taste the honey in these caramels, and it's a sweet flavor that isn't overpowering. Wrap them individually in wax paper to give out during the holidays, or put them in a gift basket for the new neighbor. They keep for up to a month when stored properly.

Generously butter a 9 × 13 baking pan. In a medium saucepan, bring the sugar, honey, and corn syrup to a heavy boil. Carefully drop ½ cup of butter into the mixture and stir until the butter melts. Slowly add the evaporated milk; pour it in a very thin line and stir continuously. Make sure the mixture stays at a boil while you incorporate the milk. Insert a candy thermometer and bring the mixture to 232 degrees. Remove the pan from the heat and add the vanilla. Pour into the prepared pan and allow to set for 3–4 hours before cutting and wrapping individually.

Ingredients

2 cups milk chocolate chips

1 cup semisweet chocolate chips

2½ cups mini marshmallows

1 (14-oz.) can sweetened condensed milk

½ tsp. vanilla

½ tsp. mint flavoring

¾ cup mint chips, divided

Mint Fudge

Makes 24 servings

The amount of mint flavoring you use may need to be adjusted according to the potency of your flavoring. My flavoring is strong, so I use a half teaspoon in this recipe. If your mint flavoring is mellow, you may want to take it up to three-fourths or even one full teaspoon. As it is written, the fudge comes out chocolate with a hint of mint.

Line a 9 × 9 pan with plastic wrap and set aside. Place the milk chocolate chips, semisweet chocolate chips, marshmallows, and sweetened condensed milk in a large saucepan. Place the saucepan on the stove over medium-low heat. Stir occasionally, scraping the ingredients off the bottom.

Once the chocolate mixture is smooth, after 10–15 minutes, remove the pan from the heat and add the vanilla, mint flavoring, and ½ cup of mint chips. Stir well and pour the mixture into the prepared pan. Sprinkle the remaining mint chips on top and place the fudge in the fridge to set.

Variation:

Peanut Butter Fudge: Add ¼ cup peanut butter with the chocolate chips, omit the mint flavoring, increase the vanilla to 1 teaspoon, and substitute peanut butter chips for the mint chips.

Salted White Chocolate Peanut Clusters

Makes 24

Ingredients

1 (12-oz.) pkg. white baking chips

2 Tbsp. shortening

1 tsp. salt

2½ cups whole peanuts

While many people love the combination of salted nuts and chocolate, some people prefer their chocolate unsalted. Feel free to use unsalted peanuts if you desire a change.

Place 24 candy cups in a mini muffin tin (or simply set them out on the counter).

Place a medium saucepan over medium-low heat. Add the baking chips and shortening. Once the chocolate is smooth, remove the pan from the heat. Add the salt and stir well. Then add the peanuts and stir to coat.

Spoon the coated peanuts into the candy cups, and allow to set before removing the cups from the muffin tin.

Upside-Down Mounds

Makes 32

Ingredients

1½ cups shredded coconut, divided

½ cup light corn syrup

12 large marshmallows

1 tsp. vanilla

½ cup powdered sugar

1½ cups semisweet chocolate chips

If you're more of a nut-with-your-candy-bar type of person, then you can sprinkle a half cup of almonds over the top of the chocolate when it melts and before it has a chance to set.

Lightly spray a 9 × 9 baking dish with nonstick cooking spray. Sprinkle ¾ cup of coconut across the bottom of the dish and set aside.

In a medium saucepan, melt the corn syrup and marshmallows until smooth. Stir often while melting. Once the marshmallow mixture is smooth, remove the pan from the heat and stir in the vanilla, powdered sugar, and remaining shredded coconut.

Immediately pour the mixture over the coconut in the prepared pan. Add the chocolate chips. Once the chips get shiny, use a knife to spread them flat. Make score marks in the chocolate, and allow to set for an hour. Cut and serve by turning upside down on a plate.

Caramel Mousse

Makes 4 servings

Ingredients

1¾ cups whipping cream

½ cup powdered sugar

1 tsp. caramel flavoring

½ cup Karo dark corn syrup

caramel, for drizzling (optional)

The trick to making a good mousse is to whip the whipping cream until you almost have butter. Do not be a wimpy whipper! What's the worst that could happen if you whipped too long? You'd have homemade butter! It's not caramel mousse, but homemade butter ain't bad. Besides, you will probably be able to stop at mousse stage once you see it. It just takes a little practice to get the right consistency. What better recipe to practice on than Caramel Mousse?

Place a mixing bowl in the freezer for 10 minutes. This works best if your bowl is metal, but ceramic can get pretty cold too. Use your cream right out of the fridge to make sure it's cold.

Pour the cold cream into the cold bowl and whip it until soft peaks form. With the beaters going, slowly add the powdered sugar one heaping spoonful at a time. Pour the caramel flavoring in all at once and beat until stiff peaks form; if you can pull your beaters out and the peak stands tall, then you've made it to mousse stage.

Once the cream is thick enough, slowly add the Karo syrup while you continue to whip. Transfer the mousse to individual-sized serving bowls. Cover with plastic wrap. Press the plastic right up to the mousse to prevent air holes. Store in the fridge until you're ready to serve. If you'd like, drizzle a little caramel topping over the individual bowls before serving.

Ingredients

½ lb. chocolate coating

1 cup trail mix,
any variety

Anything Bark

Makes 8 servings

Bark is one of the easiest types of candy to make, and it is beloved by all. If you can make bark, then you can make many other candies that simply involve melting chocolate coatings. It's a good recipe to develop some confidence in yourself and to experiment with. The chocolate coating used for this recipe is sold in the baking section of the supermarket and comes in bricks.

Place a long sheet of wax paper, wax side down, on the countertop or bread board. Fill a medium saucepan halfway full of water. Place over medium-low heat.

Break the chocolate into ¼-inch pieces. Place the chocolate into a small saucepan. Place the chocolate pan on top of the water pan, making sure the water doesn't get into the chocolate because it can cause it to freeze. You've now made a double boiler to melt your chocolate coating.

Gently stir the chocolate as it melts. Once the chocolate coating is smooth, wipe the bottom of the pan with a dish towel to remove any moisture. Pour the chocolate onto the wax paper. Use a spatula to spread it out to about a ¼-inch thickness. Sprinkle with trail mix and allow to set. Break into pieces to serve.

Variation:

You don't have to only use trail mix. You can use plain nuts, candy pieces, peanut butter cups, chopped cookies, or pretzel pieces. You can also mix half the trail mix into the chocolate before spreading it out and then sprinkle the other half on top. This is one recipe you can truly make your own.

Turtle Bites

Makes 12 bites or 4 servings

Ingredients

1 (5.5-oz.) pkg. individually wrapped caramels

1 (2-oz.) bag pecan halves

½ cup milk chocolate chips

Werther's Original caramels work best. Other caramels may need a shorter melting time. If you're using a different brand of caramel, turn on your oven light and keep a sharp eye on the turtles. You don't want to cook the caramel because it will change from soft and chewy to crunchy.

Preheat the oven to 300 degrees. Line a cookie sheet with aluminum foil. Lightly spray the foil with nonstick cooking spray.

Arrange pecan halves into star shapes—5 pecan halves per star. Make 12 stars. Unwrap 24 caramels. (If you have extra, go right ahead and pop those in your mouth. No one will ever know there were more than 24 in the package.) Place 2 caramels on top of each star. Carefully place the cookie sheet in the oven for 5 minutes.

Remove the cookie sheet from the oven. The caramel should have melted slightly and formed around the pecans. Immediately divide the chocolate chips among the turtles. Once the chocolate melts, use the back of a spoon to swirl it into a circle. Allow the turtles to cool before removing them from the cookie sheet.

Charming Cakes, Cupcakes, Cobblers & Pies

Cakes have made their way into the biggest moments of our lives. Every birthday has a cake with candles. Every wedding has a cake for the couple to feed each other small bites of (or cover one another in frosting with). Even promotions and other accomplishments at work are celebrated with cake. Seeing how cake appears at the biggest moments in our lives, it's no wonder cake has become a symbol for happy times.

Like tiny foot soldiers, cupcakes evaded cake's territory and became as indispensable as their older siblings. Individually wrapped cupcakes are great finger foods, though some creations are so decadent that they require a fork, plate, and napkin. You'll find a few of those in here.

Chocolate Cake to the Third Power (p. 110) is an especially fun cake to make and serve. The three different flavors of cake all come from one bowl. You could also use the same recipe to make an easy but ambitious-looking trifle. No one will ever know how quick it all comes together.

Ingredients

3 egg whites

1 cup sugar

1 tsp. vanilla

7 graham crackers, crushed

1 cup finely chopped walnuts

1 tsp. baking powder

1 tsp. cinnamon (optional)

whipped cream or vanilla ice cream

Graham Cracker Pie

Makes 8 servings

This pie was inspired by the candied nut stands that pop up around Christmas time. The pie is fantastic with or without the cinnamon.

Preheat the oven to 350 degrees. Spray a pie plate with nonstick cooking spray and set aside.

Whip the egg whites until stiff but not dry, 4–7 minutes. Add sugar and vanilla and beat together. Add the graham cracker crumbs, chopped nuts, baking powder, and cinnamon (optional). Mix well.

Pour batter into the prepared pie plate. Bake for 30 minutes. Top with whipped cream or serve warm with a scoop of vanilla ice cream.

Pumpkin Bundt Cake

Makes 16 servings

Ingredients

1 cup butter,
room temperature

2 cups sugar

4 eggs

1 (15-oz.) can pumpkin

⅔ cup milk

2 tsp. vanilla

1½ cups wheat flour

1½ cups flour

3 tsp. cinnamon

1 tsp. nutmeg

½ tsp. cloves

1 tsp. ginger

2 tsp. baking soda

½ tsp. baking powder

1 tsp. salt

cream cheese frosting or
powdered sugar for
dusting (optional)

The spices used when baking with pumpkin paint images of red and yellow leaves as well as warm scarves and a favorite hoodie. The secret to any bundt cake is to grease and flour the pan as if your baking reputation depended on it.

Preheat the oven to 350 degrees. Grease and flour a bundt pan and set aside. In a large mixing bowl, beat the butter and sugar until light and fluffy. Add the eggs one at a time, mixing well between each addition. Add the pumpkin, milk, and vanilla. Mix until combined, scraping down the sides as necessary.

Add the wheat and white flours, cinnamon, nutmeg, cloves, ginger, baking soda, baking powder, and salt. Beat well until the spices are evenly incorporated.

Pour the batter into the prepared pan and bake for 60 minutes, or until a toothpick inserted in the cake comes out clean. Allow the cake to cool for 15 minutes before inverting it onto a serving platter. You can frost the cake with cream cheese frosting, dust with powdered sugar, or serve alone.

Hummingbird Sheet Cake

Makes 24 servings

Ingredients

2 large ripe bananas

3 eggs

3 cups flour

2 cups sugar

1 tsp. salt

2 tsp. baking soda

1 tsp. cinnamon

½ tsp. nutmeg

1¼ cups oil

2 tsp. vanilla

1 (8-oz.) can crushed pineapple, drained

½ cup chopped walnuts

½ cup raisins

2 tubs store-bought cream cheese frosting

additional walnuts, for decoration (optional)

When it comes to serving a crowd, nothing does the job quite like a sheet cake. They mix up quickly and bake in one giant pan, and all you have to do is frost and cut to serve. This is a great cake for a baby shower or family gathering.

Grease and flour a large cookie sheet with sides and set aside. Preheat the oven to 350 degrees. Peel the bananas and place them in a large mixing bowl. Use a hand mixer to beat them until they are smooth. Add the eggs and mix on high for 1 minute. Add the flour, sugar, salt, baking soda, cinnamon, nutmeg, oil, and vanilla. Mix well. You can now add the pineapple, walnuts, and raisins.

Pour the batter into the prepared cookie sheet, spreading it evenly to the corners and edges. Cook for 25–30 minutes, or until a toothpick inserted in the center comes out clean. Allow the cake to cool, and then frost with cream cheese frosting. Garnish with additional nuts if desired.

Moist Chocolate Cake

Makes 18 servings

Ingredients

1 cup sugar

1 cup mayonnaise

2 cups flour

1½ tsp. baking powder

1½ tsp. baking soda

½ cup cocoa

1 tsp. vanilla

1 cup milk

fudge frosting

I'm not sure who came up with the idea of using mayonnaise in cake. It makes sense—mayo is basically eggs and oil whipped together, and cakes need both ingredients. What I do know is that this cake turns out moist and crumbly, and it satisfies even the toughest cake cravings.

Preheat the oven to 350 degrees. Spray a 9 × 13 baking pan with nonstick cooking spray and set aside.

In a medium mixing bowl, combine the sugar, mayonnaise, flour, baking powder, baking soda, cocoa, vanilla, and milk until the lumps are gone. Pour the batter into the prepared pan and bake for 30 minutes, or until a toothpick inserted in the center comes out clean. Once cool, frost with fudge frosting.

Upside-Down German Chocolate Cake

Makes 16 servings

Ingredients

½ cup chopped pecans

1 cup shredded coconut

2 cups sugar

1 cup butter, room temperature

½ cup cocoa

½ cup milk

1 tsp. vanilla

4 eggs

2¼ cups flour

1 tsp. baking soda

1 tsp. salt

1 cup buttermilk

caramel topping, for serving (optional)

Since the coconut and nuts are baked right into the cake, there's no need to frost this delicious adaptation. For a fabulous presentation, try swirling caramel topping across the plate before putting the cake on it. This brings just the right touch of class to an elegant cake like this one.

Preheat the oven to 350 degrees. Spray a 9 × 13 baking pan with nonstick cooking spray. Sprinkle the chopped pecans and shredded coconut over the bottom of the pan. Set pan aside.

Cream together the sugar and butter. Add the cocoa, milk, vanilla, and eggs. Beat well. Add the flour, baking soda, salt, and buttermilk. Scrape down the sides of the bowl as necessary.

Pour the batter over the coconut and pecans. Bake for 35–40 minutes, or until a toothpick inserted in the center comes out clean. Allow the cake to cool for 10–15 minutes in the pan before inverting onto a serving tray.

White Chocolate Almond Poppy Seed Cake

Makes 16 servings

Ingredients

1 Tbsp. shortening

½ cup chopped white chocolate

½ cup butter, room temperature

1¼ cups sugar

4 egg whites

2 cups flour

¾ cup milk

1 tsp. vanilla

1 tsp. almond flavoring

½ tsp. salt

2 tsp. baking powder

2 Tbsp. poppy seeds

powdered sugar for dusting or white chocolate frosting

This cake is good as a bundt cake or as a layered cake. The directions for both are included below.

Preheat the oven to 350 degrees. Grease and flour a bundt cake pan or two 8-inch round pans. Set aside.

In a medium-size, microwave-safe mixing bowl, melt the shortening and white chocolate on half power for 1 minute. Stir and then return to the microwave for 30-second intervals, stirring after each interval until the chocolate is smooth.

Add the butter and sugar and mix well. Add the egg whites. Scrape down the sides of the bowl and make sure the mixture is smooth before adding the flour, milk, vanilla, almond flavoring, salt, baking powder, and poppy seeds. Once the batter is smooth, pour it into the prepared pan(s).

Bake the bundt cake for 45–50 minutes or the 2 rounds for 25–30 minutes, or until a toothpick inserted in the center comes out clean. Transfer the cake(s) to a wire rack to cool before dusting with powdered sugar or frosting with white chocolate frosting.

Caramel Cake with Pecan Frosting

Makes 12 servings

Ingredients

4 eggs

1¾ cups sugar

¾ cup butter, room temperature

1 cup milk

1 tsp. vanilla

2 tsp. caramel flavoring

3 cups flour

4 tsp. baking powder

1 tsp. salt

2 (16-oz.) containers cream cheese frosting

1 cup pecan frosting

caramels and caramel sauce, for garnish (optional)

This three-layer cake is deceptively easy. When you look at it, it looks like it took all day—in reality, it comes together super quick.

Preheat the oven to 350 degrees. Grease and flour 3 (8-inch) round cake pans. Set aside.

Beat the eggs for 1 minute in a large mixing bowl. Add the sugar, butter, milk, vanilla, and caramel flavoring. Add the flour, baking powder, and salt. Beat until smooth, about 2 minutes. Divide the batter evenly among the 3 pans. Bake for 25–30 minutes, or until a toothpick inserted in the center comes out clean. Transfer cakes to a wire rack to cool.

Once cool, level the cakes. Place one layer on a cake stand and frost with a thin layer of cream cheese frosting. Add second layer of cake and frost again. Add third layer of cake. On the top of the cake, pipe frosting in swirls around the edge of the cake. This will create a well for the pecan frosting. Spread pecan frosting over the center of the cake. Garnish with caramels and caramel sauce if desired.

Blueberry Ribbon Cake

Makes 12 servings

Ingredients

1¾ cups sugar

⅔ cup shortening

2½ cups flour

1 cup milk

¼ cup water

3½ tsp. baking powder

½ tsp. salt

2 tsp. clear vanilla

5 egg whites

1 cup blueberry pie filling, divided

whipped cream

When trying to create swirls in cake batter, it's best to make cuts vertically and then horizontally. Remember that the batter will most likely look more swirled once the cake is cooked and cut than it does staring down at it. If you over-swirl, you'll end up with a blotchy cake instead of a swirled cake.

Preheat the oven to 350 degrees. Grease and flour two 9-inch round pans and set aside.

Beat together the sugar and shortening until fluffy. Add the flour, milk, water, baking powder, salt, and clear vanilla. Add the egg whites, mixing well and scraping down the sides of the bowl as needed.

Divide the batter equally between the 2 pans. Place 4 tablespoons of blueberry pie filling on the top of each pie pan of batter. Reserve the remaining pie filling for serving. Drag a knife through the batter to create swirls. Bake for 28–30 minutes, or until a toothpick inserted in the center comes out clean.

Once the cakes are baked, run a knife around the inside edge of the cakes to loosen them from the pans. Transfer the cakes to wire racks and allow them to cool before frosting with whipped cream and drizzling with the remaining blueberry pie filling.

Cheesecake Sundaes

Makes 12 servings

Ingredients

12 ice cream cups

1 (8-oz.) pkg. cream cheese, room temperature

¼ cup sugar

1 egg

½ cup sour cream

½ tsp. vanilla

½ cup mini chocolate chips

hot fudge (optional)

caramel topping (optional)

whipped cream (optional)

mini chocolate chips for garnish (optional)

Do your cheesecakes turn out lumpy? It's most likely because your cream cheese is too cold. In order to get those creamy cheesecakes you crave, let your cream cheese come to room temperature. You can set it out overnight as long as it is sealed in the package.

Preheat the oven to 325 degrees. Use a muffin tin to stand the ice cream cups upright. Set aside.

Beat the cream cheese in a medium mixing bowl until it's creamy. Add the sugar and beat again. Add the egg, scrape down the sides, and beat until smooth. Add the sour cream and vanilla. Stir in the mini chocolate chips.

Divide the batter among the 12 ice cream cups. Bake for 45–50 minutes, or until the centers are set.

Allow to cool in the fridge for at least 1 hour before topping with your favorite flavors and serving.

Mint Valley Cupcakes

Makes 24

Ingredients

24 mint-flavored cream-filled cookies

2 cups flour

1⅓ cups sugar

¼ cup dark cocoa

3 eggs

⅔ cup milk

¼ cup oil

1 tsp. vanilla

1 tsp. baking soda

½ tsp. salt

1 cup crème de menthe baking chips

chocolate frosting

mint chocolate candies

A mint sandwich cookie wrapped in dense chocolate cake and topped with fudge frosting is the perfect finish to any meal—or the perfect three o'clock snack. (A.m. or p.m.—you can take your pick.)

Preheat the oven to 350 degrees. Line a muffin tin with cupcake liners. Drop 1 mint cookie in each muffin liner. Set aside.

In a medium mixing bowl, lightly stir together the flour, sugar, and cocoa. Add the eggs, milk, and oil, and mix well. Add the vanilla, baking soda, and salt. Stir until the batter is smooth. Fold in the baking chips.

Divide the batter among the cupcake liners, filling them three-fourths full. Bake for 22–25 minutes, or until a toothpick inserted in the center comes out clean.

Frost with chocolate frosting and top with mint chocolate candies.

White Chocolate and Strawberry Cupcakes

Makes 24

Ingredients

4 egg whites

1½ cups sugar

¾ cup butter, room temperature

1 cup milk

3 cups flour

4 tsp. baking powder

1 tsp. salt

1 (3.3-oz.) pkg. white chocolate pudding mix

½ cup strawberry filling

2 cups whipped cream

These cupcakes can be described with one word: delightful. The mixture of white chocolate and strawberry tastes like summertime and running through the sprinklers. They're great for barbecues because you don't have to serve them on plates, and the wrappers can be thrown away with the rest of the paper goods.

Preheat the oven to 350 degrees. Line a muffin tin with muffin cups and set aside.

In a medium mixing bowl, beat together the egg whites, sugar, and butter until light and fluffy. Add the milk, flour, baking powder, salt, and pudding mix. Beat until batter is smooth, for about 2 minutes, scraping down the sides of the bowl as necessary.

Divide the batter among the cupcake cups, filling them half full. Bake for 18–20 minutes, or until a toothpick inserted in the center comes out clean. Transfer to a wire rack to cool.

Once cupcakes are cool, cut a small cone-like section out of the top. Fill the hole with strawberry filling. Add a dollop of whipped cream to the top of the cupcake and serve.

Plum Upside-Down Cupcakes

Makes 12

Ingredients

2 Tbsp. butter, cut into 12 pieces

12 tsp. brown sugar

12 tsp. white sugar

3 plums, peeled and cut into 4 pieces each

¾ cup butter, room temperature

¾ cup sugar

¼ cup brown sugar

¼ cup sour cream

2 cups flour

1 tsp. baking powder

½ tsp. salt

2 eggs

2 tsp. vanilla

whipped cream (optional)

The term "upside-down cake" was first printed in the 1920s, although the cakes themselves had been around for decades. The earliest versions all used fruits native to the region of the cook or chef because they were the easiest to acquire.

Preheat the oven to 350 degrees. Grease and flour a muffin tin. Place 1 piece of butter, 1 teaspoon of brown sugar, 1 teaspoon of sugar, and 1 piece of plum into each muffin cup. Set aside.

Combine the ¾ cup of butter, sugar, brown sugar, and sour cream in a mixing bowl. Add the flour, baking powder, salt, eggs, and vanilla. Mix well. Divide the batter into the muffin cups.

Bake for 22–25 minutes, or until a toothpick inserted into the center comes out clean. Allow the cupcakes to cool for 5 minutes. Run a knife around the edge of each cupcake. Place a platter on top of the muffin tin, hold them both together, and then flip the whole thing over so the cupcakes come out of the pan and onto the platter. Remove the muffin tin. Serve warm or cold. Top with whipped cream if desired.

Ingredients

1 cup butter, room temperature

½ cup cocoa (mild, not dark)

2 cups sugar

4 eggs

1½ cups flour

½ tsp. salt

1½ cups chopped walnuts, divided

1 (10-oz.) bag mini marshmallows

fudge frosting

Grandma's 24-Hour Cupcakes

Makes 24

These cupcakes can be made up to 24 hours in advance. In fact, because it takes the marshmallows a few hours to set, it's better to make them the day before your gathering. If you do that, don't frost them until right before you serve them, but make sure to keep them covered so they don't dry out.

Preheat oven to 350 degrees. Line a muffin tin with cupcake liners and set aside.

Beat the butter, cocoa, and sugar in a medium mixing bowl. Add the eggs one at a time, mixing well after each addition. Add the flour and salt and mix again. Stir in 1 cup of walnuts.

Divide the batter among 24 cupcake liners. Bake for 20–25 minutes, or until a toothpick inserted in the center comes out clean. Remove the pan from the oven and cover each cupcake with marshmallows. Return the pan to the oven and bake for 5 minutes, or until the marshmallows puff but do not brown. Allow the cupcakes to cool completely and then frost with fudge frosting and sprinkle with the remaining walnuts.

Vanilla Peach Bundt Cake

Makes 12 servings

Ingredients

¾ cup butter, room temperature

¼ cup sugar

3 eggs

2 Tbsp. vanilla

¾ cup vanilla yogurt

2 cups flour

1 Tbsp. baking powder

½ tsp. salt

2 cups chopped fresh peaches (about 3 medium peaches)

This cake is sweet. It doesn't need any garnish, but if you simply must dress it up, top it with whipped cream and additional peaches.

Preheat the oven to 350 degrees. Grease and flour a 10-inch bundt cake pan. Set aside.

In a medium mixing bowl, cream the butter and sugar. Add the eggs one at a time. Add the vanilla and vanilla yogurt. Mix until the batter is smooth. Add the flour, baking powder, and salt. Stir in the peaches.

Pour the batter into the prepared pan and bake for 45–50 minutes, or until a toothpick inserted in the cake comes out clean.

Allow the cake to cool for 10–15 minutes before inverting it onto a serving platter.

Ingredients

1 cup butter

¾ cup sugar

1 tsp. vanilla

½ cup pumpkin

1 egg

½ tsp. baking soda

½ tsp. salt

1 tsp. pumpkin pie spice

1½ cups flour

2 graham crackers, divided

18 marshmallows, cut in half

cream cheese frosting

Inside-Out Pumpkin S'more Cupcakes

Makes 12

Pumpkin is traditionally associated with fall. However, this delicious flavor doesn't have to wait for the leaves to turn colors. These s'more cupcakes are sure to become a family favorite.

Preheat the oven to 350 degrees. Spray a muffin tin with nonstick cooking spray and set aside.

Melt the butter in a medium-size, microwave-safe mixing bowl. Add the sugar and mix well. Add the vanilla, pumpkin, and egg. Sprinkle the baking soda, salt, and pumpkin pie spice over the top of the batter. Add the flour and mix until the batter is no longer lumpy.

Cut each graham cracker into 8 pieces. Place 1 piece in the bottom of each of the 12 muffin slots. You'll have 4 graham cracker pieces leftover—set them aside for later. Divide the batter among the cups in the muffin tin. They should be two-thirds full. Bake for 15–18 minutes, or until a toothpick inserted in the center comes out clean.

Allow the cupcakes to cool for 10 minutes. Cut each cupcake in half to make a top and bottom. Place the bottoms on a cookie sheet. Place 3 marshmallow halves on each cupcake bottom. Place the cookie sheet in the oven for 5 minutes, or until the marshmallows expand and begin to brown.

Remove the pan from the oven and place the tops of the cupcakes on top of the marshmallows. Allow to cool completely, and then frost with cream cheese frosting. Crush the remaining graham crackers and sprinkle the crumbs over the frosting.

Chocolate Cake to the Third Power

Makes 12 servings

With white chocolate, milk chocolate, and dark chocolate layers covered in vanilla frosting, this cake is sure to please every type of chocolate lover and then some.

Ingredients

1 (18.25-oz.) box white cake mix

1 (5.9-oz.) box white chocolate pudding

1 cup sour cream

1 cup oil

4 egg whites

½ cup milk

¼ cup cocoa

1½ Tbsp. special dark cocoa

vanilla frosting

Preheat the oven to 350 degrees. Grease and flour three 8-inch round cake pans. Set aside.

In a large mixing bowl, combine the cake mix, pudding, sour cream, oil, egg whites, and milk until the batter is smooth. Spoon 2 cups of batter into a cake pan. Set aside.

Add the ¼ cup cocoa to the remaining batter. Stir until well incorporated, making sure to scrape down the sides of the bowl so all the white batter is mixed in. Transfer 2 cups of batter into a second cake pan and set aside.

Add the special dark cocoa to the remaining batter. Stir until well incorporated, making sure to scrape down the sides of the bowl so the milk chocolate batter is mixed in. Pour the batter into the last cake pan.

Transfer all the cake pans to the oven and bake for 25–30 minutes, or until a toothpick inserted in the center comes out clean.

Once the cakes are baked, run a knife around the edges of the cakes to loosen them. Allow the cakes to cool for 10 minutes and then transfer them from the cake pans to wire racks to cool. Once cool, stack the cakes with the dark chocolate on the bottom, the milk chocolate in the middle, and the white chocolate on top, using the vanilla frosting between the layers and on top.

Peach Cobbler

Makes 16 servings

Ingredients

½ cup butter

2 cups sugar, divided

2 cups flour

4 tsp. baking powder

¼ tsp. salt

1 cup milk

1 (15-oz.) can peaches

An oldie but a goodie, peach cobbler is a favorite for any type of gathering. Since it is scooped to serve, you don't have to worry about it looking beautiful; it's truly a low-stress dessert.

Preheat the oven to 375 degrees. Spray a 9 × 13 baking pan with nonstick cooking spray and set aside.

In a medium mixing bowl, cream the butter and 1 cup of sugar. Add the flour, baking powder, salt, and milk, and beat until smooth. Spread the batter into the prepared pan. Arrange the peaches over the batter, but save the juice for the finishing step. Sprinkle the remaining cup of sugar over the top of the peaches and then pour the juice from the peaches over the top of the whole thing. Bake for 45 minutes.

It's best to let it cool for 10–15 minutes before serving. You can eat it plain or add a scoop of vanilla or pecan ice cream.

Blender Pumpkin Pie

Makes 8 servings

Ingredients

4 eggs

2 cups milk

1 cup sugar

1 cup canned pumpkin

½ cup flour

¼ cup butter

1 tsp. vanilla

1 tsp. cinnamon

¼ tsp. nutmeg

¼ tsp. cloves

⅛ tsp. salt

2 (9-inch) premade pie crusts

whipped cream, for topping

The easiest pumpkin pie ever made! You don't even need a bowl—just a blender. You can use a regular pie crust or a graham cracker pie crust; both work equally well.

Preheat the oven to 350 degrees. Place the eggs, milk, sugar, pumpkin, flour, butter, vanilla, cinnamon, nutmeg, cloves, and salt in a blender. Blend on low speed for 15 seconds. Divide the batter evenly between the 2 pie crusts. Bake for 45–50 minutes, or until the pies are set and a knife inserted in the center comes out clean. Place the pies in the fridge to set, for 2 hours, and top with whipped cream to serve.

Cooking Measurement Equivalents

Cups	Tablespoons	Fluid Ounces
⅛ cup	2 Tbsp.	1 fl. oz.
¼ cup	4 Tbsp.	2 fl. oz.
⅓ cup	5 Tbsp. + 1 tsp.	
½ cup	8 Tbsp.	4 fl. oz.
⅔ cup	10 Tbsp. + 2 tsp.	
¾ cup	12 Tbsp.	6 fl. oz.
1 cup	16 Tbsp.	8 fl. oz.

Cups	Fluid Ounces	Pints/Quarts/Gallons
1 cup	8 fl. oz.	½ pint
2 cups	16 fl. oz.	1 pint = ½ quart
3 cups	24 fl. oz.	1½ pints
4 cups	32 fl. oz.	2 pints = 1 quart
8 cups	64 fl. oz.	2 quarts = ½ gallon
16 cups	128 fl. oz.	4 quarts = 1 gallon

Other Helpful Equivalents

1 Tbsp.	3 tsp.
8 oz.	½ lb.
16 oz.	1 lb.

Metric Measurement Equivalents

Approximate Weight Equivalents

Ounces	Pounds	Grams
4 oz.	¼ lb.	113 g
5 oz.		142 g
6 oz.		170 g
8 oz.	½ lb.	227 g
9 oz.		255 g
12 oz.	¾ lb.	340 g
16 oz.	1 lb.	454 g

Approximate Volume Equivalents

Cups	US Fluid Ounces	Milliliters
⅛ cup	1 fl. oz.	30 ml
¼ cup	2 fl. oz.	59 ml
½ cup	4 fl. oz.	118 ml
¾ cup	6 fl. oz.	177 ml
1 cup	8 fl. oz.	237 ml

Other Helpful Equivalents

½ tsp.	2½ ml
1 tsp.	5 ml
1 Tbsp.	15 ml

Index

H

I

L

M

N

O

P

R

S

T

U

V

W

ALSO BY CHRISTINA DYMOCK

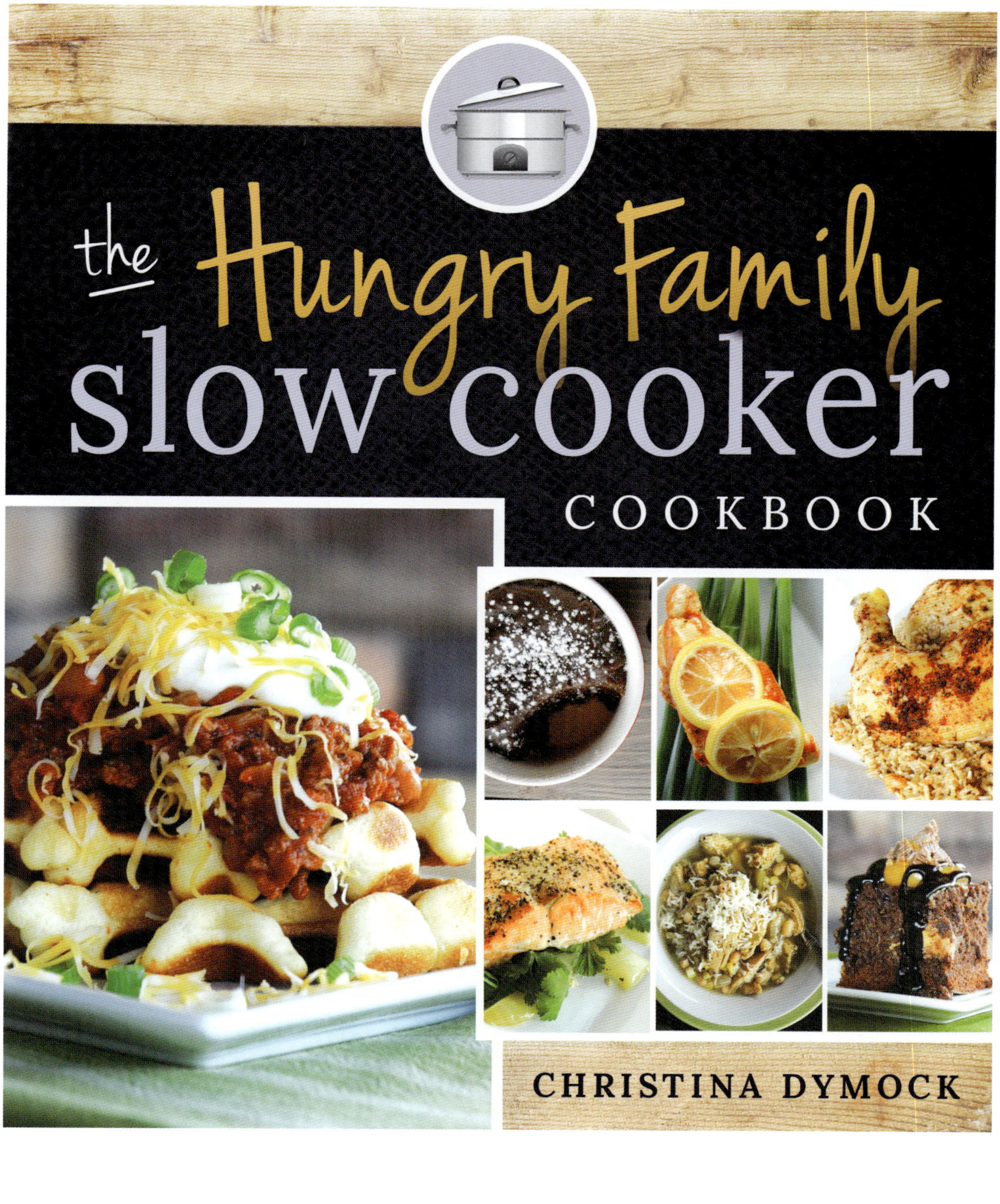

ALSO BY CHRISTINA DYMOCK

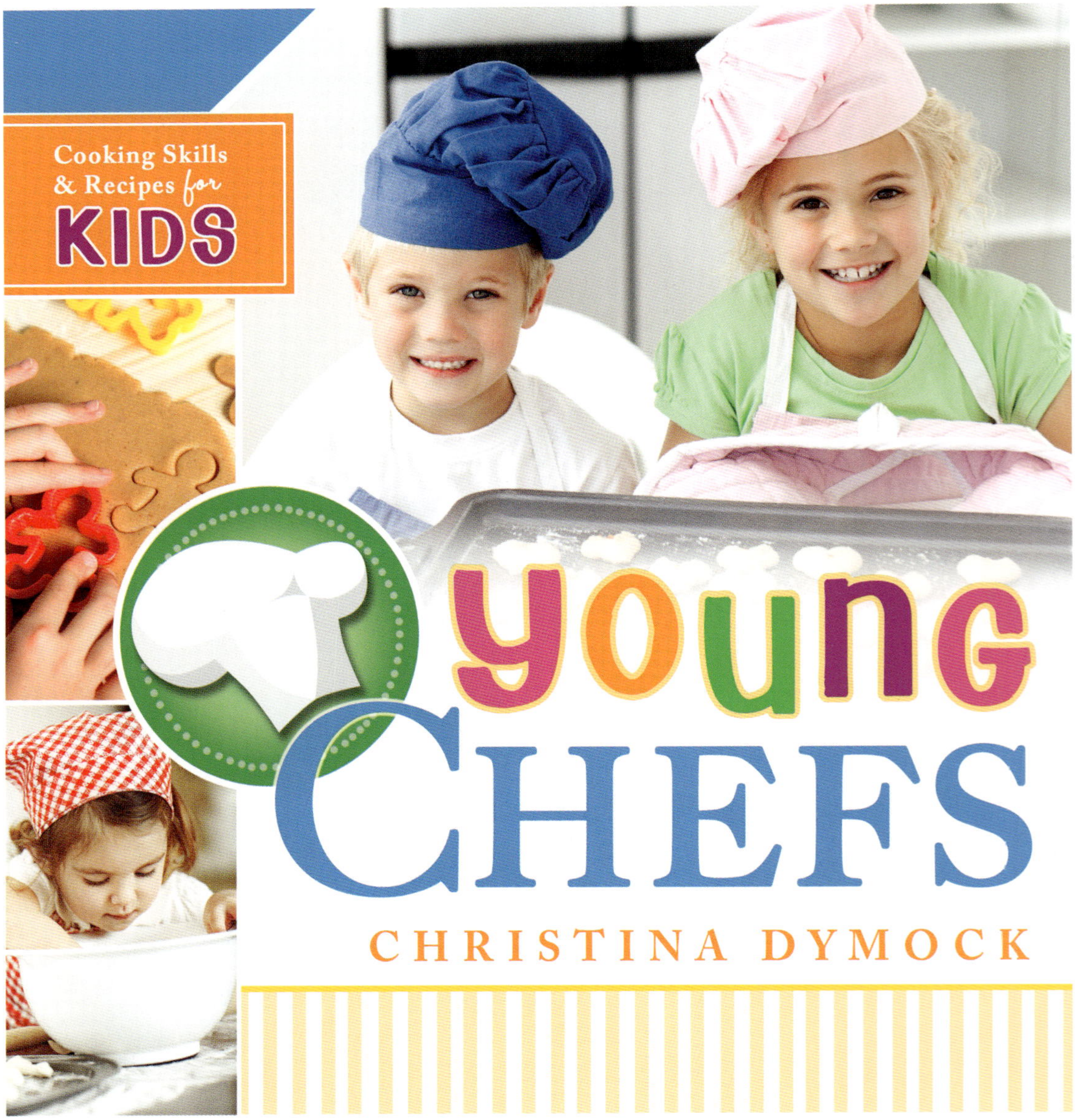

About the Author

Christina Dymock graduated from the University of Utah with a bachelor's degree in public relations. She has been published in *Woman's World* magazine and in several Chicken Soup for the Soul books. She is also the author of *101 Things to Do with Popcorn*, *Young Chefs: Cooking Skills & Recipes for Kids*, and *The Hungry Family Slow Cooker Cookbook*. She resides in central Utah with her husband and four children.

You can follow their cooking adventures at
TheHungryFamilyatHome.com

Praise for One dirty BOWL

"As a busy mother of five and a cookbook author, I dirty a load of dishes daily. With recipes from *One Dirty Bowl*, I now can whip up a delicious dessert in minutes while only dirtying one bowl. That is a win-win for everyone. Spending less time in the kitchen means more time with my family. Bravo for *One Dirty Bowl*."

Shauna Evans, author of *Sweet and Savory*, *Skinny-licious*, and *30-Minute Meals for Families*

"From cookies to brownies to mini cakes and cheesecake, *One Dirty Bowl* is full of sweet little bites that are perfect for the busy dessert-lover! It's a delicious go-to!"

Courtney Whitmore, pizzazzerie.com, author of *Frostings*, *Push-up Pops*, and *Candy Making For Kids*

0 26575 14016 3